The Milford Series
Popular Writers of Today
Volume Fifty
ISSN 0163-2469

The Second Marxian Invasion
The Fiction of the
STRUGATSKY BROTHERS

by
Stephen W. Potts

BORGO PRESS / WILDSIDE PRESS

www.wildsidepress.com

*　　*　　*　　*　　*　　*　　*

Library of Congress Cataloging-in-Publication Data

Potts, Stephen W., 1949-
The second Marxian invasion : the fiction of the Strugatsky Brothers / by
Stephen W. Potts.
    p. cm. — (The Milford series, popular writers of today, ISSN 0163-
2469 ; vol. 50)
    Bibliography: p.
    Includes index.
    ISBN 0-89370-179-3 : $22.95. — ISBN 0-89370-279-X (pbk.) : $12.95
    1. Strugatskii, Arkadii Natanovich—Criticism and interpretation. 2. Stru-
gatskii, Boris Natanovich—Criticism and interpretation. 3. Science fiction,
Russian—History and criticism. I. Title. II. Series.
PG3476.S78835Z84 1991   84-309
891.73'0876'09—dc19   CIP

CONTENTS

A STRUGATSKY CHRONOLOGY

1925 Arkady Natanovich Strugatsky born on August 28 in Batumi, Soviet Georgia, son of Natan Strugatksy and Aleksandra Litvinchova.

1933 Boris Natanovich Strugatsky born on April 15 in Leningrad, Russian Federated Soviet Socialist Republic.

1949 Arkady graduates from the Military Institute of Foreign Languages, Moscow.

1955 Boris graduates from the Mechanics and Mathematics College of Leningrad State University.

1957 First publication of the Brothers' first story, the novella *Land of Crimson Clouds*.

1960 Publication of their first book, the collection *Six Matches*, gathering short stories originally published from 1957 to 1959, and a second collection, named for the featured novella, *Destination Amaltheia*.

1962 Publication of *The Homecoming (Noon: 22nd Century)*, another short story collection, as well as *The Apprentices* and *An Attempted Escape*. First American appearance of the Strugatskys with publication of the story "Spontaneous Reflex" in the anthology *Soviet Science Fiction*.

1963 Publication of *Far Rainbow*.

1964 Publication of *Hard To Be a God*; the novel quickly becomes a best-seller among Soviet SF readers.

1965 Publication of *Predatory Things of Our Time* and *Monday Begins on Saturday*. Latter becomes another best-seller, while the former elicits critical controversy in the Soviet press because of its depiction of a decadent capitalist state in the future.

1966 Publication of "Kandid" half of *Snail on the Slope* in the Soviet anthology *Ellenski sekret*.

1967 Expanded version of *The Homecoming* published as *Noon: 22nd Century*.

1968   Publication of "Pepper" half of *Snail on the Slope* in provincial magazine *Baikal*, as well as *The Second Martian Invasion* and *Tale of the Troika*, bringing conservative attacks on the authors. The scheduled publication of *Ugly Swans* is cancelled at the last moment. *Snail on the Slope* and *Ugly Swans* then appear in unauthorized editions in Germany.

1970   Magazine publication of *Hotel "To the Lost Mountaineer."*

1971   *The Inhabited Island* and novella *The Kid* are published.

1973   First American publication of the Strugatskys' novels, *Second War of the Worlds* (Macmillan) and *Hard To Be a God* (Seabury Press).

1974   DAW publishes *Hard To Be a God*, the first American paperback of a Strugatsky novel.

1977   DAW publishes *Monday Begins on Saturday*; Macmillan/Collier publishes *Noon*, *Prisoners of Power*, *Tale of the Troika*, and *Roadside Picnic*, marking the initiation of their reprint program of Soviet science fiction.

1980   *Snail on the Slope* is scheduled for publication by Bantam, and printed and distributed, but is withdrawn at the last moment when the Strugatskys protest the marketing of the novel as a product of dissidents; some copies do find their way into bookstores.

1984   The Soviet movie *The Stalker*, based loosely on *Roadside Picnic*, is released.

1987   *The Time Wanderers* published in Great Britain by Richardson & Steirman.

1988   *The Time Wanderers* reprinted in the U.S. by St. Martin's Press.

I.

THE STRUGATSKY BROTHERS IN CONTEXT

If one asked the average science-fiction fan in the English-speaking world who are the most widely read authors of science fiction on the planet, the answer would probably be Isaac Asimov or Ray Bradbury, or perhaps Arthur C. Clarke or Robert A. Heinlein. It is doubtful that most readers would mention Polish author Stanislaw Lem, or the Russian brothers, Arkady and Boris Strugatsky. Yet these Eastern Europeans have been translated and published nearly as widely as Asimov and Bradbury, and they are at the top of the reading list among millions of fans in the former Soviet bloc. In the past decade, Lem has caught the attention of Western academics; he has even appeared in such mainstream periodicals as *The New Yorker,* and his works have been compared, in their blend of realism and fantasy, to those of Franz Kafka, Vladimir Nabokov, and Jorge Luis Borges.

Arkady and Boris Strugatsky have not yet entered the international literary mainstream, perhaps because their work is more clearly rooted in the traditions of the science fiction genre, or perhaps because, unlike Lem, they frequently delve into political and dialectical matters. Particularly in their early work, this dialectic has a distinct Marxist flavor. But while it is a dominant element in their fiction—and especially interesting in the philosophical evolution that takes place over the course of their careers—it is not the only element. The Strugatskys couple their political concerns with artistic ones, treating their readers to a variety of styles, themes, and genres—from space adventure to surreal satire to cosmic mystery.

The foundations of the Strugatskys' work can best be understood through a brief overview of the history of science fiction in the Soviet Union.

Historical Context

As in Western Europe, the first glimmerings of science fiction in Russia arose from the fantasy voyage, the idea of utopia, and political satire, often in combination. For the most part, these tended to endorse the already existing tsarist autocracy. Thomas More's *Utopia*, not published in Russia until the French Revolution, had its sixteenth-century tsarist counterpart in *The Legend of Sultan Mahomet* by Ivan Peresvetov, an oriental tale promoting Ivan the Terrible's push for state centralization. In the eighteenth-century wake of Peter the Great, several Russian writers extolled enlightened absolutism, a movement which climaxed in Mikhail Shcherbatov's incomplete *Voyage to the Empire of Ophir*. The era of revolution at the century's end brought more liberal, democratic visions to the fore, such as Alexander Radishchev's *Journey from Petersburg to Moscow*, and caused Catherine the Great to suppress the entire genre.

Not until the 1820s did political fantasy return to Russia, through the pen of official propagandist Thaddeus Bulgarin. His 1825 *Untrue Un-Events, or a Voyage to the Center of the Earth* posits three subterranean countries, one, Ignorance, inhabited by benighted peasants, another, Beastliness, ruled by middle-class pseudo-intellectuals, and the third, Enlightenedness, another aristocratic utopia. This work was followed by Bulgarin's *True Un-Events, or Voyages in the World of the 29th Century*, which, new to the nineteenth century, set utopia in the future rather than in an exotic country. Prince Vladimir Odoevsky, a progressive if anti-bourgeois aristocrat, brought the genre up-to-date in the 1840s with his unfinished *Year 4338*. Although he takes for granted the continuation of tsarist absolutism and hierarchy, he predicts radical advances in science and technology. Among his prognostications are air and space travel, electric illumination and communication, plastic clothing, and the artificial heating of the Arctic.

Given the progressive urges of the nineteenth century, it was inevitable that the growing belief in technological progress would be accompanied, even in politically backward Russia, by the desire for social reforms. After the failed Decembrist revolt of 1825, radicals in Russia found their voice in utopian fiction of a more democratic bent. Most influential was Nikolai Chernyshevsky's *What Is To Be Done?* (1862), written in a tsarist prison and released only by bureaucratic error. Its romantic, utopian heroine, Vera Pavlovna, unites personal and political liberation in her love life and her vivid dreams of a libertarian socialist paradise. Chernyshevsky's vision of the possible inspired a generation of disaffected Russians, while giving the revolutionary apostate Dostoevsky much material to respond to; dark burlesques of Chernyshevsky's matter and manner can be found in *Notes from the Underground*, *Crime and Punishment*, and *The Possessed*, and his own inverted wish-fulfillment, *The Dream of a Ridiculous Man*.

Another small surge in utopian feelings and writings accompanied the relaxation of official suppression in the first decade of the twentieth century. With a glance westward at the contemporary social science fiction of Wells and London, in 1904 symbolist poet Valery Bryusov wrote the play *Earth*, in which a revolt of young radicals destroys a glass dome enclosing a decadent metropolis. His 1907 *Republic of the Southern Cross*, on the other hand, is a dystopia about a plague ravaging a similarly decadent domed city, its fatalism probably in part a result of the failed 1905 revolution. Bryusov would reappear with other dark, if more optimistic visions after the revolution.

Of the few other stories in the Wellsian vein that appeared in Russia before the October Revolution, most noteworthy are those of maverick Bolshevik Alexander Bogdanov (Malinovsky). His *Red Star* (1908) sets the Marxian utopia on Mars and, in its blend of love story and workers' paradise, set the standards for the Soviet planetary tale for decades thereafter. He followed it up in 1913 with *Engineer Menni*.

Other Russian writers, perhaps responding to translations of the more technological fiction of Jules Verne, produced scientific speculations of their own, including a technically oriented future history in N. Komarov's *Coldtown*. Along this line the most significant works of the pre-revolution era were the first slender volumes by mathematician and rocket theorist Konstantin Tsiolkovsky: *On the Moon* and *Daydreams of Earth and Heavens*. His speculative fictions would not take hold, however, until Lenin's transformation of Russian society. Tsiolkovsky's best work, *Outside Earth*, appeared the year after the October Revolution, and he quickly became the mentor for a generation who wished to take humankind, and the revolution, into space.

Lenin, himself an avid reader of utopian literature, saw in science fiction a method for popularizing the whole idea of radical political and technological progress. With his active encouragement, speculative fiction flourished in the Soviet Union in the 1920s, producing what could be called the first Marxian invasion of the genre. In contrast to the scant 25 original works of Russian SF that appeared in the twenty years before 1917, six or seven times that many showed up in the decade following. Most were optimistically utopian, envisioning future worlds of classic, classless Marxist societies. The best and most influential of these was produced by respected author Alexei Tolstoy. His 1922 *Aëlita*, showing the influence of Edgar Rice Burroughs as well as London, Wells, and the Bogdanov of *Red Star*, sets the revolution on Mars and counterpoints a bittersweet romance between a rocket scientist and a Martian princess. With *Aëlita*, Russian SF finally received world attention and entered the literary mainstream. In honor of this pivotal novel, the chief Soviet science fiction award—corresponding to the American Hugo and Nebula—is called the "Aëlita."

Alongside of these revolutionary romances ran the also common catastrophe novels, targeting the decadence and recalcitrance of the non-Marxist world. A blend of Vernean technological prediction with Wellsian social disaster, they posit capitalist oligarchies brought down by the abuse of the proletariat and the misuse of robots, chemical and biological warfare, and "deathrays." Here again the best example of the form is a work by Alexei Tolsoy, *The Garin Death Ray*, originally serialized as *Hyperboloid of Engineer Garin* in 1925-26. It places an amoral scientist in the middle of a thriller plot, competing for power through atomic control in a capitalist society, though doomed like it to defeat at the hands of the masses.

Even authors in the Soviet mainstream at this time produced many works that fit the genre, if only marginally. Most popular of such writers was Vladimir Mayakovsky, a poet who also wrote propaganda pieces and film scenarios. Best remembered for their contribution to speculative fiction were his plays, particularly *The Bedbug* (1928) and *The Bath* (1929), in which he satirizes, respectively, the bourgeoisie and bureaucracy. Mayakovsky, where he uses actual science at all, elevates it to metaphor; in *The Bath*, a time machine pits Einstein's relativity against the intransigence of bureaucrats. Ironically, Mayakovsky's real-time battle with bureaucracy led to his suicide in 1930. His reputation survived him, however, to inspire his contemporaries, such as Yevgeny Zamyatin, as well as the later generation of Soviet satirical fantasists and SF authors that included the Strugatskys.

The best-known Russian science fiction author—indeed, perhaps the best-known Russian author of any stripe—from this period is Zamyatin, the creator of *We*. In many respects the model for all subsequent dystopias of the twentieth century, and most explicitly for Orwell's *1984* and Rand's *Anthem*, *We* first appeared in the twenties, though not in the Soviet Union. Zamyatin's Bolshevism was too libertarian for the Soviet bureaucracy; though he bitterly denounced the West and capitalism, the author also decried centralized states and power elites in general. If Mayakovsky's struggle against the Soviet bureaucracy led to his death, Zamyatin's produced his exile in 1931 and the erroneous conclusion in both Eastern and Western circles that the author was a counterrevolutionary. On the contrary, Zamyatin's complaint against the Bolsheviks was that they had not gone far enough; like his utopian predecessors from Chernyshevsky on, he desired a liberation that linked the personal (including the sexual) to the political.

More successful as a science fiction author, and still read in some circles even today, was Alexander Belyaev. He was the first Russian to make a living writing only SF, and in his twenty novels and several stories showed the influence of both Verne and Wells. He was fond of the theme of romantic alienation, often in tandem with biological alterations, as in his first novel *Professor Dowell's Head* (1925), about a brain transplantation; along similar lines are his well-remembered *The Amphibious Man* (1928), obviously concerning a human altered for underwater life, and the 1941 *Ariel*, with a protagonist given the ability to fly.

Unfortunately, the revolutionary zeal that had given Russian science fiction its Golden Age under Lenin was smothered as Stalin asserted his power at the end of the twenties. The same political contraction that prompted Mayakovsky to take his own life and that forced Zamyatin out of the country cast its pall over the entire genre. Like the tsars before him, Stalin was made nervous by the social experimentation endorsed by utopian writers. The ranks of science fiction novelists and playwrights were decimated by imprisonment and executions. Once he had reined in the scientific and social idealists, Stalin reduced SF to a sterilized, juvenile genre concerned only with the technological marvels of the near future, such as radar, improved tractors and oil drills, and the taming of the Arctic. Soviet science fiction entered its Dark Age. Authors like Belyaev survived only by reducing their technological miracles to the level of fairy tale fantasy and by injecting their work with starkly ideological thriller plots.

The renaissance came in 1956, when the Twentieth Party Congress turned Soviet society from the strict path of Stalinism. The next year Sputnik opened space up to humankind. In the flurry of enthusiasm that followed this spectacular achievement, a readership hungry for stories of the future found what they sought in a new wave of Soviet writers, the so-called "warm stream" or "Yefremov school."

Ivan Yefremov, a scientist himself, had been writing SF for some time before the thaw, but his work was considered by the dominant conservative "cold stream" in SF to be too distant from the present and too "mystical" to be publishable. The altered climate of the late fifties, however, made possible the appearance of his novel *Andromeda*.

Andromeda harked back to the utopianism of the 1920s. In it, Yefremov depicts a universe some centuries hence in which humanity maintains a ring of communication with a number of intelligent races. Although Earth has achieved a humanist, socialist perfection, individual men and women still have to face the technical and emotional problems of life in space. Yefremov's characters, though clearly superior human beings, still suffer their interludes of doubt and pain. Unfortunately, if somewhat more than human, they are somewhat less than believable, and by literary standards Yefremov often falters in characterization, motivation, and tone. In *Andromeda* as in his other work, he too frequently falls back on theatrical effects or mere preaching. Nevertheless, Yefremov changed the face of Soviet science fiction, breathing new life into the genre, inspiring a new generation of writers, readers, and critics, and unleashing the second Marxian invasion of international SF.

The ideological battle that raged in critical circles after *Andromeda* was won for Yefremov and the "warm stream" by the overwhelming popularity of the new school and by several forceful new critics. The belief grew that science fiction's purpose transcended the mere technological forecasting of the near future. To be good, science fiction had to possess literary quality and a humanist perspective as well:

> ...we take as a criterion in assessing the value of a work everything that promotes the development of the human personality, extends its horizon, inspires it with lofty ideals, ennobles it morally and intellectually, improves its aesthetic preception [sic] of the environment, helps to gain an insight into the good and evil of this world, and to respond to them more keenly—in short, it is everything that promotes the truly human in man. [E. Brandis and V. Dmitrevsky, "In the Land of Science Fiction," *Soviet Literature* (no. 5, 1968): 148.]

Perhaps no statement better summarizes the view of Arkady and Boris Strugatsky. As Yefremov's most successful disciples, they became the focus of much of the critical controversy between "warm stream" and "cold stream."

Critical Context

From the beginning of their careers, the Strugatsky brothers have found themselves at the center of critical and ideological discussions in their own country. After Yefremov, they were held up as the most representative authors of the new "warm stream" by both supporters and detractors. In the first surge of critical attention between 1959 and 1962, friends praised the realism and humanity of their characters, while conservatives charged that they were too crude and earthy, too prone to slang and colloquial language; if Yefremov's heroes were so lofty as to be unbelievable, those of the Strugatskys were barely heroic at all. When the Strugatskys themselves finally replied to such complaints in a magazine article published in 1961, they pointed out that the ideal communist of the future would, one would hope, not be smug, sententious, and boring.

They pressed this point home in a 1962 discussion in print with their "cold stream" opposition, with much success. Thereafter, influential Soviet critics of the period such as Andreev and Gromova placed the Strugatsky brothers high on their lists of important new writers, and Andreev himself provided the article that prefaced their 1962 collection. That year the Strugatskys also received their first reading in the United States, when English translations of two early stories—"Spontaneous Reflex" and "Six Matches"—appeared respectively in the anthologies *Soviet Science Fiction* and *More Soviet Science Fiction*, to praise by Isaac Asimov.

For a time after 1962, the Strugatskys appeared to have the critical consensus in their favor. As they pushed past the utopianism of their early universe to new territory in the relatively ambivalent and problematic works *Far Rainbow* and *Hard To Be a God*, they received the enthusiastic critical endorsement of Gromova and new critics Nudelman and Revich. On the other hand, science fiction writer/satirist Anatoly Dneprov, himself a transitional figure between "cold stream" and "warm stream," publicly disapproved of the new trend in the brothers' fiction, so much so that he himself abandoned the genre.

Hard To Be a God, a blend of science fiction, sword-and-sorcery, and social criticism, quickly became the Strugatskys' most popular work, followed by the 1965 *Monday Begins on Saturday*, although the latter's inclusion of broadly satiric and folkloric elements confused some moderate critics. However, not until the publication that same year of *Predatory Things of Our Time* (published more than a decade later in the U.S. as *The Final Circle of Paradise*) did the "cold stream" return to the offensive. These critics took umbrage in the depiction of a decadent capitalist state of the future, mostly on the ideological grounds that such a state would not exist in the official communist future. Granted that the novel was relatively weaker than the brothers' other work (see Chapter 2 below), the same must be said of the arguments mounted by their detractors, most of whom did not even belong to the science fiction community.

Between 1966 and 1968 there was a break in the output both of the Strugatskys and of their critics, marked by a scant handful of attacks and defenses; the most eloquent of the latter was the Strugatskys' own 1967 statement of purpose in an interview in the journal *Foreign Literature*. This relatively quiescent period was framed by the disparate appearances of the two halves of *Snail on a Slope* (see Chapter 3 below)—the surreal "Kandid" half in 1966 and the satirical "Pepper" half in 1968. Then a new controversy erupted over the Kafkaesque machinations of the bureaucracy depicted in "Pepper," which some saw as an attack on the Soviet system. Similar, if less overt, charges were rumored about their other stories of that year, the also satirical *Second Martian Invasion* and *Tale of the Troika* (discussed in Chapter III). It has struck Western critics as evidence of official disapproval that the Strugatskys' somewhat dark novel *Ugly Swans*, also scheduled for 1968 release, was abruptly cancelled. On the other hand, that year the brothers continued to receive respectful attention in bibliographical essays published in official organs in the Soviet Union and in Soviet publications aimed at foreign consumption.

In the novellas *Hotel "To the Lost Mountaineer"* and *The Kid*, the Strugatskys appeared to retreat to the relatively safe territory of their science fiction mystery stories of a decade before. But with *The Inhabited Island* (later published in the U.S. as *Prisoners of Power*), the difficult issues of ideology and social development rose to the fore again. The arguments surrounding the brothers' work continued, but less now in the public press than in symposia and exchanges conducted in background literary circles. A final compromise was achieved in

Britikov's 1970 bibliographical discussion of Soviet SF, which praises and defends their opus up to the point where, as in *Snail on the Slope*, it strays too far from the norm.

It was at this point, at the beginning of the seventies, that Western critics joined the controversy. A pair of Austrian critics, attempting to lay it out for readers in Western Europe and America, set the tone for the subsequent discussion by highlighting the Strugatskys' ideological differences with Soviet officialdom and emphasizing the political to the virtual exclusion of the literary. The first major salvo in the United States came in a 1970 article by Marc Slonim in the *New York Times Book Review*; however, in the course of asserting that the Strugatskys' satire made them dissidents, he stumbled over a number of factual inaccuracies that suggested an excessive reliance on hearsay and an unfamiliarity with the real issues of the controversy in the Soviet Union.

The allegation that the Strugatskys were dissidents, officially disapproved of and even persecuted by the Soviet bureaucracy, undoubtedly had something to do with the sudden interest taken in their fiction by Western publishers. In the mid-seventies, almost ten years after the original appearances of the novels in the Soviet Union, the American paperback company DAW Books published *Hard To Be a God*, *The Final Circle of Paradise (Predatory Things of Our Time)*, and *Monday Begins on Saturday*. Beginning in the late decade and continuing into the early eighties, Macmillan/Collier brought out virtually all of their other works—from *Noon: 22nd Century* to the late *Roadside Picnic*—in a well-packaged, well-advertised series of hardbound, trade paper, and pocket books. In 1980, Bantam attempted to bring the Strugatskys' work to the broader science fiction market with its paperback publication of *The Snail on the Slope*; their original marketing strategy—playing on the alleged dissidence of the authors—backfired, however, when the Strugatskys themselves protested and insisted that the book be withdrawn.

Given the sudden bounty of the Strugatskys' fiction in translation, academic critics in the West began to direct their attention to the Soviet brothers. Darko Suvin, a Slavist based at McGill University in Montreal, had paved the way in the early seventies with a pair of bibliographical articles on the Strugatskys' fiction published in the scholarly journal *Canadian-American Slavic Studies*. Circa 1980 academic editors and publishers made arrangements for a handful of studies and essay collections concerning the Strugatskys, although the first of these are appearing only now, a decade later. In the meantime, articles on specific topics have appeared in a range of other scholarly venues; 1986, for instance, saw a discussion by István Csicery-Ronay, Jr., in *Science-Fiction Studies*, of the brothers' use of fairy tale motifs and a feminist critique by Diana Greene of *The Snail on the Slope* in *Modern Fiction Studies*, while the Soviets themselves devoted a large part of one of that year's issues of their English language journal *Soviet Literature* to the Strugatskys. These and other recent essays shall be addressed at greater length where appropriate below.

For the most part academics subscribe to the dominant Western view that the Strugatskys were officially in disfavor with the Brezhnev government; as Greene notes in passing in the article mentioned above, "No doubt political considerations have prevented the reprinting of *The Snail on the Slope* in the USSR. In the 1960s the Strugatskys' use of science fiction to write thinly veiled criticisms of the Soviet government made them controversial figures" (*Modern Fiction Studies*, Spring 1986, p. 99).

From the foregoing, it is evident that the Strugatskys originally stimulated much animated discussion in the Soviet press. Whether they are regarded as dissidents by Soviet authority, however, or whether they regard themselves as such, is much less certain than many Western critics would have it. The Soviet press continues to advance the brothers in print as the nation's foremost science fiction writers, and Arkady has, on and off, continued to function as a major editor in Soviet SF publishing. He is given the frequent opportunity of interviews in Soviet publications, where his pronouncements tend to match the themes of his fiction.

In one such interview, with Alexander Fyodorov in a 1983 number of *Soviet Literature*, the elder Strugatsky brother cites as his major literary influences Alexei Tolstoy, Mikhail Bulgakov, and Yefremov, and refers to Ray Bradbury, Stanislaw Lem, Kobo Abe, Kurt Vonnegut, Robert Sheckley, and Ursula K. Le Guin as science fiction writers who deserve the respect of the international literary establishment. To the question of SF ideology, Arkady observes

> Soviet science fiction is the child of the great revolution, and that explains its mission and its special features. Our science fiction is socially and ideologically committed and humane....Its ideal is communist humanism and it approaches all problems from this an-

gle....It fosters an active mentality, a kind of mentality that is intolerant of narrow-minded bourgeois atti-
tudes. (*Soviet Literature*, 122).

Shortly thereafter he insists that "to portray us the critics of
'the Soviet regime,' internal émigrés and dissidents, is the ultimate in
absurdity....One can't help being amazed at the wild mixture of stupidity, arrogance and ignorance of the 'champions of freedom for Soviet
writers' who are spreading, out of ignorance or ill will, clichés that are
insulting to Soviet writers" (123). One could pass off such strong
statements as borne of necessity; others have maintained that here, as
elsewhere, Arkady is speaking ironically. If in fact dissidents, however, the Strugatskys do an excellent job of concealing their desire to
overthrow the Soviet system. Slavist Patrick L. McGuire, on the other
hand, asserts that the Strugatsky brothers "are, and more particularly,
were when they started writing, exactly what they present themselves
as—mildly liberal Marxist-Leninists" ("Future History, Soviet Style,"
Critical Encounters II, ed. Tom Staicar, Ungar 1982; p. 106).
      Whatever their political status in their native country, the So-
viet Union has continued to publish the brothers' work and promote it
in publications produced for foreign consumption. Official estimation
of their careers cannot be too dissimilar from the pronouncements of the
Great Soviet Encyclopedia: while noting that many of their works,
such as *Snail on the Slope*, "aroused criticism and polemics in the
press," this official Soviet publication concludes rather approvingly that
"[t]he Strugatsky brothers defend the humanist ideal of progress, warn
against soulless prosperity, attack oppression, and reflect on the role of
the individual in society and on man's responsibility for the future" (v.
24, p. 605).
      The social and political content of the Strugatskys' fiction
merits discussion primarily because, in its mature phase anyway, it re-
jects the orthodoxies of *either* side in the Cold War dispute. Unfortunately, here as in their own country, the ideological controversy has
tended to eclipse the esthetic concerns of the brothers' work. This
study will attempt to redress the balance by placing political and artistic
matters in perspective relative to one another. Given their status in the
world science fiction community, the career of the Brothers Strugatsky
deserves an objective evaluation.

17

II.

THE ROAD TO UTOPIA

The very earliest stories of the Strugatskys were hard-core puzzlers, much in the same vein as the contemporary *Analog* school of the 1950s. Such a piece is "Spontaneous Reflex," in which an otherwise well-behaved robot breaks out of its laboratory prison and creates havoc in the research compound, but only—it is finally determined—in response to its programming; the machine's innate function, as one destined to go where man cannot, is to explore and learn.

In another widely reprinted story from the late fifties, "Six Matches," a scientist risks his life and sanity by experimenting with neutrino beams directed at his own brain. On the verge of developing superhuman powers, he suffers a mental breakdown. A careful perusal of his notes and the evidence of lab assistants suggests that the scientist collapsed while attempting to lift a bundle of six matches via telekinesis. The official in charge of the investigation chastises the scientist *in absentia* for his "barbarous heroism." Stating a position that will recur frequently throughout the Strugatskys' early work, the inspector argues that there are limits to scientific research, particularly when human lives are involved:

> The human race should gain mastery over nature not by sacrificing its best sons but by using powerful machines and precise instruments. Not simply because the living could accomplish far more than the dead but because Man was the most precious thing in the world. [*Soviet Literature* (no. 5, 1968): 85].

Their first major works, however, appeared as a loose trilogy from 1960 to 1962. *Strana bagrovykh tuch* (*Land of the Crimson Clouds*), "Put an Amaltheia," ("Destination: Amaltheia"), and *Stazhery* (*Probationers*) lead a set of overlapping characters through adventures

19

in the solar system. The last work, translated into English as *Space Apprentice*, brings to a close the careers of the cycle's protagonists, spacefarers Yurkovsky, Bykov, and Dauge. As the climactic work of the trilogy and the only one now widely available in English, it is worth examining in detail.

Like the earlier stories in the cycle, *Space Apprentice* takes place at the end of the twentieth century, at which time it is assumed communism has pulled peacefully ahead of capitalism—economically, politically, and scientifically—and is leading the push into space. Earth itself, though still far from solving all its problems, is well along towards the socialist world state and the material and spiritual well-being that should imply. But pockets of capitalism, gangsterism, philistinism, and parasitism yet exist wherever human beings reside, on Earth or in space.

The framework for this episodic novel, parts of which were originally published as short stories, is an inspection voyage undertaken by Yurkovsky, a planetologist who has just become the Inspector-General of the International Administration of Cosmic Communications (IACC), the organization that oversees space exploration/exploitation. He permits one Yura Borodin, an eighteen-year-old vacuum welder who had missed his Saturn-bound construction junket, to come along on the trip as an apprentice; the reader experiences most of the narrative through Yura's senses and sensibilities. During the course of the voyage, the ship—the *Takhmasib*—will make stops at Mars, in the asteroid belt, and at the rings of Saturn. Most of the action sequences take place at these stops, each of which imprints a new lesson on Yura. The stretches in between are filled with philosophical ruminations and the petty details of shipboard life.

Despite Theodore Sturgeon's contention (in his introduction to the 1981 Macmillan edition) that this novel contains very little Marxism, it is in fact wholly dialectical. The dialectics treat not only the obvious issue of communism and capitalism, however, but the subtler if related matters of common good vs. individual good and of professionalism vs. heroism, a theme already touched on in "Six Matches."

The subject of communism, capitalism, and the greater good of humankind comes into sharpest relief in the book's two central chapters. In Chapter 8 ("Einomia. The Death Planeters"), Yurkovsky visits a cramped and woefully undersupplied research lab in the asteroid belt where the scientists, despite the hardships they suffer, are a frankly jolly and ambitious lot, "real men in the process of real work." In contrast, the world of the next chapter ("Bamberga. The Poor in Spirit") is a capitalist horror, an asteroid mining colony where the workers, all Westerners, make a fortune for themselves and their company mining precious stones for rich ladies back on Earth, though in the process absorbing so much harmful radiation that they are doomed to sterility, or at best badly deformed children, and early death.

The settlement is a hotbed of vice—gambling, bootlegged liquor, violence, and the most obvious forms of materialism and "philistinism," defined here as "the obliqueness of the petty person." The ruling commissar, a Hungarian named Bela, has been overwhelmed by his charge and has retreated into depression and alcohol, even as he continues to defend communist ideology. In one long and friendly argument with the Western engineer Sam, Bela links communism with idealism, optimism, and humanism, capitalism with greed, consumerism, and a pragmatic but short-sighted pessimism. For the capitalist Sam, "Man is cattle by nature. Give him a filled food trough, no worse than his neighbors, let him stuff his belly, and give him the opportunity to laugh once a day over some simple-minded show" (Macmillan, p. 136). Bela replies that in capitalist societies men are brought up to be cattle, and that with the right education future generations will be immune to philistinism and fascism.

In this episode, we see the ideological battle reach a dramatic resolution with the appearance of Inspector-General Yurkovsky. Yurkovsky confronts the gangster-boss of the company office, Richardson, and puts him under arrest. Richardson calls to his defense an angry mob of workers and thugs. Shots ring out as Richardson hypocritically prays to his God. Yurkovsky, unperturbed, shouts the miners down, has all weapons confiscated, and makes it quite clear that the outpost will either bow to the laws of humanity or be dismantled. The chapter ends soon thereafter on a typically optimistic note. After lamenting the animal behavior of these "small businessmen," Yurkovsky wonders if the workers could elect "someone more or less decent" to succeed Richardson as director. As if on cue, the miners' spokesman Joshua shows up at the door to return a handful of precious stones Yurkovsky had left behind. Redemption is possible even among the worst of men.

Another aspect of the personal vs. collective good argument that runs through the narrative is the familiar issue of heroism. The novel comes down decidedly in support of the view that heroics are self-indulgent and usually a waste of human life. The issue dominates the story's climax. Leading up to it is an exchange between Yurkovsky and the cautious ship captain Bykov about the former's recklessness, on Bamberga and elsewhere. This is followed by a discussion between Yura and his middle-aged mentor Zhilin about heroics. Zhilin insists that the heroic characters of adventure stories are too simple; real human life is too complex to allow people to throw away their lives out of adolescent romanticism. Yura faces the matter directly when the *Takhmasib* reaches the rings of Saturn. Yurkovsky, still a planetologist at heart, persuades Bykov to allow him to explore the rings in a small, vulnerable shuttle. But as Bykov had feared, Yurkovsky forces the craft into danger when he pursues what seems to be an alien satellite. The vehicle is damaged, and both Yurkovsky and his navigator are killed. Their discovery drops out of the narrative as Yura struggles to deal with the painful loss of his comrades. He soon arrives at Zhilin's opinion that no heroic deed is worth a human life.

It is this intense humanism that underlies all the themes of the novel, best expressed in the character Zhilin who, during the course of the narrative, decides he wants to give up space travel to become an Earth-bound teacher of children:

> He could teach them to want many things simultane-
> ously and to want to work at full speed. Teach them
> not to bow to authority, but to study it and compare
> its teachings with life; to treat the experiences of peo-
> ple with caution, because life changes with startling
> speed; to despise philistine wisdom. Teach them that
> skepticism and cynicism in life are cheap, that it's a
> lot easier and more boring than being eternally sur-
> prised and pleased by life. Teach them to trust the
> feelings of their neighbors. Teach them that it's better
> to be wrong about a person twenty times than to treat
> everyone with suspicion; that it's not how others in-
> fluence you, but how you influence others; and that
> one person alone isn't worth a damn. [p. 170]

This sentimental wisdom is characteristic of the book's tone, which is positive, humane, hopeful, and not a little didactic. The authors take a definite stand in favor of the common good and common goodness. They see the truest and best form of heroism in hard, satisfying work, work performed for the benefit of all; the struggling but hearty researchers of Einomia are such heroes of labor. And they find, like the warmhearted Zhilin, the real future of humankind in its children, children who must be educated to expect the best from themselves and their fellows.

Given the relatively straightforward approach of the novel and its adolescent hero, it is probable that *Space Apprentice* was written for the young male audience that must have formed the core of SF readership in the Soviet Union in the fifties. The Strugatskys, however, apparently set out to write a distinct kind of adolescent story, not the typical "drama with chases, exploits, and self-destruction" referred to in the narrative, but "the drama of human souls, subtle emotions, which is more complex, fascinating or tragic than anything else...." [p. 166]. It cannot be said that the authors succeed in doing this; although they do balance dramatic episodes with more thoughtful passages and a few subtle observations of character, the novel is too blatantly instructional to pass itself off as a work of emotional complexity. In the end, the authors leave all the important questions answered.

A science fiction writer working within a strict Marxian framework has one important constraint: every vision of Earth's future must take into account the imminent success of utopian socialism (as outlined in the following chapter). In such an ideal world, human conflict is reduced, to paraphrase the Strugatskys, to a battle between the good and the better. In the near-future universe of *Space Apprentice*, a few pockets of capitalism and philistinism remain, but even these are attributed to miseducation rather than inherent evil. Furthermore, the inevitability of the outcome—in every episode, the "good guys" win—contributes an element of blandness to the narrative, at least for the sophisticated reader.

The Strugatsky brothers proved themselves adept at working within the parameters of this future in their next major opus, *Polden' XXII vek*—in English, *Noon: 22nd Century*. In its final form, this volume brought together twenty stories written circa 1960. On the whole, it is a much better work than *Apprentice*, more varied, more intelligent, and often rich in subtleties, although the overall message remains the same. It begins in the world of the late twentieth century, overlapping the Yurkovsky universe, but focusing on an entirely different set of characters, characters whose interwoven lives span two centuries of human development.

Noon depicts the sunny midday of this cycle of history. Warfare, crime, capitalism, and other historic social ills are things of the recent past; the people of East, West, North and South have all of their material needs—food, shelter, transportation, etc.—well-fulfilled and are reaching out to the planets in this solar system and others. Mars is being settled, Venus terraformed, and archeological evidence of an ancient alien intelligence has been discovered both on and about the red planet (Deimos and Phobos are artificial satellites) and on another world orbiting a distant star. Yet all is not quite perfect in the utopia of the twenty-second century, and people are still people with very human problems.

The book is divided into four parts. The first, entitled "Almost the Same," is comprised of two stories set in the near future. The opening tale, "Night on Mars," concerns a trek across the Martian landscape by two men who are going to deliver the first baby born on the planet. It is primarily an adventure story, focusing on the dangers of the "flying leeches," predatory creatures exterminated in the Martian sequence of *Apprentice*. The piece ends, however, on a note of wonder and promise at the prospect of the imminent birth and the eventual domestication of Mars.

The second story, the one which lends its title to this section, moves ahead to the early twenty-first century and an academy that trains space explorers. It details a brief impediment in the education of cadet Sergei Kondratev, who has been temporarily forbidden to progress in centrifuge training and thus fears he may be permanently bound to Earth duty. Complicating his emotional response is a recent break-up with a girlfriend. Eventually, the gentle, self-sacrificial prodding of his friend Panin, who calls into question the need for and practicality of space travel, drives Kondratev to an angry recommitment to his future. Both stories introduce a motif that will recur throughout *Noon*: obstacles to human progress are limited in effect and duration; despite personal setbacks, the better world of the future continues its unstoppable approach.

The second section of *Noon*, "Homecoming," pursues the history of Sergei Kondratev and Evgeny Slavin (the child born in "Night on Mars") as they fulfill a prophecy of the aforementioned Panin by arriving in the mid-twenty-second century after the long disappearance of their near-light-speed ship. Pursuant to the prophecy, they find themselves, after 150 years of Einsteinian space-time travel, relics of the past on an Earth alien to them. It is a lovely Earth, however, united under a single socialist government, able to provide for the material well-being of all its inhabitants, and no longer ravaged by humankind's historical ills. In the absence of these, the human species can apply all its energies to pushing back the frontiers of science.

Of the nine stories in this section, all but one deal with the arrival and adjustment of the two men in this new world. The ebullient Slavin, whose medical training is, of course, obsolete, quickly finds a new career as a historian and journalist. For navigator Kondratev, however, the task of creating a place for himself in utopia is much more difficult. A trilogy of tales, the best three in this section, documents his struggle to belong. In "Two from the *Taimyr*," we see Slavin making a hospital visit to Kondratev, who is still convalescing from the crash landing of their ship. Slavin tells the melancholy Kondratev of his work, of his new girlfriend, and of the wonderful world that waits outside. After Slavin leaves, Kondratev tries to imagine this Earth he has not yet seen, seriously doubting his ability to adapt to it as well as Slavin. What pains him most is not having an active role in this society; reflecting the Marxist work ethic, Sergei longs to feel useful, to contribute something to the collective good through meaningful employment. The authors add a last typical touch of hope, as Kondratev opens his eyes from deep thought to find his doctor sitting beside him and telling him, "Everything will be all right, Sergei."

Finally out on his own in "The Moving Roads," Kondratev explores his new environment by mounting one of the slow-moving pedestrian conveyors that cross the park-like countryside. He discovers that the "great-grandchildren," as Slavin calls them, are not so different from the people of the Earth he left behind: they play, work, laugh, and argue; they express happiness, sadness, and anger. Just as he is wondering why anyone would want such a gradual means of transportation as the moving roads, Sergei enters a city where he encounters a massive statue of Lenin on a granite block, "straining ever forward...his arm [stretched] out over this city and this world, this shining and wonderful world that he had seen two centuries before" [Macmillan, 1978; p. 88]. The suggestion, of course, is that this much better, if not yet perfect, world was foreseen by Lenin—indeed, owes its existence to him. In fact, one could view the moving road, with its deliberate but definite forward movement, as a metaphor for Marxist-Leninism and, more broadly, human progress.

Sergei eventually falls in with a group of young people in a dining hall who are discussing the settlement of Venus. In the last scene of the story, he is staring at the planet in the night sky, wondering if his future lies there, aching to be doing something useful. His thoughts are echoed by an unnamed companion who reminds him that the generation of that day is energetic and unstoppable, adding, "The interplanetary expansion of the human race is beginning—like the discharge of some giant electric potential" [p. 96].

Kondratev finally finds his new role in society in "Homecoming," the last story of the section. It opens with Sergei sulking in his apartment after having spent the morning searching for a new profession. He receives a visit from one Leonid Gorbovsky, a lanky, lethargic, good-natured man who introduces himself as a "spacer." They discuss a number of things, such as Sergei's crash landing on a far planet and the settlement of Venus, in a way that suggests a cautious note in Gorbovsky's approach to space exploration. Gorbovsky finally gets around to the main point of his visit: introducing Kondratev to the oceanographer Zvantsev, who shows up more or less on cue. A large, hearty man, Zvantsev invites Kondratev to join him in the watery universe of Earth's oceans, tending plankton or whales, doing research, having adventures. It all sounds attractive to Sergei who, again consistent with the Marxist work ethic, exults to himself, "*Work....Here it is—real work!*" As a worker, he now genuinely belongs to the twenty-second century.

The sole story in this section that does not concern Slavin and Kondratev is "The Conspirators," a light, sentimental piece about four bright, adventurous schoolboys who plot to escape from their dormitory and slip aboard a ship to Venus. The teacher who supervises them gets wind of the plot, however, and gently foils it by getting the conspirators occupied in scientific puzzles, one of them, significantly, the composition of *ignis fatuus*. The teacher sincerely loves and cares for his children (as do all right-thinking adults), touching once more on a major theme in the Strugatskys' fiction: children are humanity's most important resource, because they are our future.

"The Conspirators" introduces, as characters or as names, the figures who will dominate the third and longest section of the book, "The Planet With All the Conveniences." The head of "the conspirators," Genka Komov, later becomes a planetologist and administrator along the lines of the Yurkovsky of the earlier cycle. Co-conspirator "Athos" Sidorov—intelligent, haughty, and, as his nickname suggests, something of a romantic—also seeks a career in space exploration. The remaining two, the genial Sasha Kostylin and the witty Pol Gnedykh, grow into other roles. The men they most study and admire—Gorbovsky, Zvantsev, Dr. Mboga—all appear in stories of their own in section three.

The first story in the section, "Languor of the Spirit," brings Pol and Sasha together as men in the prime of life. While Sasha Kostylin does important research at a large agricultural commune, Pol Gnedykh (whose last name sounds suspiciously like the German *gnädig*, meaning "gracious") has fallen upon hard times, professionally and spiritually. He is suffering from a "languor of the spirit," rooted in an inability to stick to one job for very long. Adding to his discomfort is a recent unsuccessful love affair. His alienation is much like that experienced in the last section by Sergei Kondratev, confirming Sergei's discovery that the people of that century, despite their utopian surroundings, still confront many of the personal problems of ages past. Through most of the story, Pol wanders through the compound, his observations interspersed with glowing advertisements for the future.

This story touches but lightly on the main matter of this section, the uses, misuses, and personal dimensions of scientific research. Some more representative pieces are "Deep Search," which documents Kondratev's no-nonsense attitude toward his new profession, "Candles Before the Control Board," in which a grueling effort by a team of scientists makes personal immortality feasible, and "The Assaultmen," which contrasts "Athos" Sidorov's romantic attitude toward space exploration with the cautious, thoughtful professionalism of Gorbovsky and his first officer Mark Falkenstein. All of these give emphasis and variety to the already familiar motif of commonplace heroism, a job well done in the service of human progress.

A few stories do not offer such clear-cut lessons. One, "The Mystery of the Hind Leg," is something of a joke; in it Slavin investigates the mysterious appearance of several bizarre cybernetic devices, only to discover that they are the product of misplaced graduate student zeal. Another is the ironic "Pilgrims and Wanderers." Unique in being the only first-person narrative in the volume, it details a casual encounter between the speaker, a crusty, middle-aged underwater technician named Ivanov, and Leonid Gorbovsky. Ivanov's current assignment is to electronically tag a newly discovered terrestrial life-form called "septipods." These squid-like creatures became known only when they left their deep-sea domain to invade estuaries, freshwater bodies, and even dry land, for as yet obscure reasons. Gorbovsky, vacationing beside the lake where Ivanov works, finally draws the analogy between septipods and human beings.

They stayed in the depths for ages, and now they've risen up and entered an alien, hostile world. And what drives them? An ancient, dark, instinct, you say? Or an information-processing capacity which had risen up to the level of unquenchable curiosity? After all, it would be better for it to stay home, in salt water, but something draws it...draws it to the shore. [p. 251]

While this discussion has been going on, Ivanov's daughter has been having difficulty with her radio, which is picking up interference of some sort. Gorbovsky makes the startling confession that the radio noise is coming from him. Since his last mission he, his crew, and his ship have all been emitting the same signal for no apparent reason anyone can determine. It is as if he and the rest have been "tagged" as well by some unidentified extraterrestrial intelligence. Ivanov, however, is privately unimpressed. "They could hardly find us all that interesting," he remarks—an ironic statement in view of his own current concerns. Like "Hind Leg," this less serious piece lacks the ideological edge of most of the stories. Instead, it looks ahead to a theme that would dominate the Strugatskys' fiction of a decade or more later, the confrontation with the truly alien (discussed in Chapter IV below).

Bringing this section to a thematic close is its title story, "The Planet With All the Conveniences." Written as a scientific puzzler, it takes place on a planet of great, apparently natural, beauty and harmony with only one mysterious trace of intelligent life, a collection of primitive huts. Eventually, however, we learn that the planet's entire ecosystem is a tribute to its elusive native humanoids; they have made a paradise of their world simply through selective breeding. Komov, who heads the expedition, decides along with the zoologist Mboga and the rest of their party to leave this Edenic planet alone, almost grateful for an excuse not to exploit it with their noisy and destructive machines. Noteworthy is that up to this story, the term "planet with all the conveniences," appeared to refer to Earth. Even though Earth's technology retreats before this paradise, a subtle implication remains that humankind, like the humanoid species of this planet, may well, in time, create a paradise of its own.

The same implication underlies the short final division of the book, "What You Will Be Like." Each of its three stories emphasizes in a different way the distance humanity has yet to travel in order to fulfill its potential. The section as a whole, despite a touch of melancholy, points toward the probability, if not certainty, of that fulfillment.

The first story of the three, "Defeat," focuses on a middle-aged Sidorov, who has spent his career grounded on Earth due to the reckless behavior of his early manhood, as manifested in "The Assaultmen." Here, he is given the unheroic job of overseeing two "greenhorns" during a trial of a new mechanism constructed for planetary research. Called an "embryomech," it is capable of building any structure it has been programmed to build using the raw materials of its landing site. During the initial test, however, the mechanism burrows into an ammunition cache left over from the Second World War and explodes. Ironically, a harbinger of man's glorious future has been destroyed by a relic of his unseemly past. But as Sidorov recalls Gorbovsky saying, defeat "was always really only an accident, a setback which you could surmount." Typically, the authors provide a touch of optimism to an otherwise gloomy tale.

Something similar happens in "The Meeting," another tale featuring Pol Gnedykh and Sasha Kostylin, now also older. Pol has obviously found himself a niche since the earlier story, as a hunter of zoological specimens on other planets. In this short episode, Pol is making what has become a ritual visit to the museum where his preserved specimens are displayed. He is there to do penance before one particular trophy, the facial fragment of a creature that had exploded on one volatile world when he shot at it. Only later did he realize that he must have destroyed an alien explorer also visiting the planet. For years Kostylin has tried to convince him that, as a zoologist and taxidermist, he knows it was just an animal, but he finally admits to Pol at the story's conclusion, by silently tracing the word *sapiens* on the display plaque, that he too had known the truth. In its simplicity and subtlety, this is a sensitive, unsettling, and powerful piece.

The story that concludes the volume, "What You Will Be Like," brings together Gorbovsky and the twenty-first century ex-spacers Kondratev and Slavin. As the three men fish and camp on the shore of a Terran sea, they begin, in the now familiar fashion of the characters in *Noon*, to speculate about the future. The discussion is initiated by mention of the first contact with a living alien civilization, which Gorbovsky will soon be visiting under the auspices of a Contact Commission headed by Komov. From there Gorbovsky proceeds to an anecdote about a strange visitation he and his comrade Falkenstein experienced on a recent voyage. Their ship was in trouble and they had given themselves up for dead when a man suddenly appeared, healed their mortally wounded shipmate, and returned the vessel to perfect running order. After other superhuman feats, he informed them that he was a human being from the future, a descendent there to show his ancestors "what they will be like" and to encourage them to keep "on course."

Though it appears from the dialogue that follows that the anecdote is actually a fabrication, the men take its message seriously. They believe themselves to be the progenitors of Supermen, the stuff of an ultimately omnipotent race of beings. Slavin's final words to Gorbovsky, and the last complete observation of the book, links humanity's progress to the teachings of Lenin:

> Lenin's idea about the development of the human race in spirals has always struck me. From the primitive communism of the destitute, through hunger, blood, and wars, through insane injustices, to the communism of endless material and spiritual wealth. I strongly suspect that this is just theory for you, but I come from a time when the turn of the spiral was not yet completed....You see, the human race began with communism and it returned to communism, and with this return a new turn of the spiral begins, a completely fantastic one. [p. 319]

While these infrequent paeans to Lenin may seem jarring to the skeptic, on the whole *Noon*'s positive portrayal of the future is convincing and attractive. The pathos, pain, conflict, irony, and burlesque required of interesting literature have not been sacrificed here in the interest of dialectic. As in the case of Yurkovsky's death in *Apprentice*, the authors prove themselves competent in the Marxist mode of "optimistic tragedy," with tales like "Defeat" and "The Meeting" that leave the reader saddened but not totally drained of hope. They show a degree of skill across a wide range, from straight-forward humor and action stories to complex yet understated philosophical and psychological sketches. And it is in the latter that they excel.

Though written at almost the same time as *Apprentice*, *Noon: 22nd Century* is a significant artistic step forward—more varied, less didactic, and in many ways both affective and thought-provoking. It

30

still occasionally bears the marks of the juvenile genre, though not nearly so much as the brothers' earlier work. The book restates the favorite themes of this period—the nature of heroism, the inevitability of progress, the desirability of work, the value of children, and the worth of the individual—and touches on a few that will come to dominate the Strugatskys' fiction later, such as the incomprehensibility of the alien.

This stage of the Strugatskys' career reaches its culmination in *Dalekaia Raduga—Far Rainbow*. First published in 1963, this short novel effectively marks the end of the Gorbovsky universe. A mature work, it lacks the obvious Marxist-Leninism didacticism of the earlier works even as it pursues the now-familiar themes of the conflict between individual and common good, the nature of heroism, and the social and moral consequences of scientific research.

"Rainbow" is a colonized planet orbiting a distant star, a world given over largely to research into "zero-physics." This branch of science circumvents the normal laws of energy and matter conservation, and Rainbow has proven to be a particularly suitable laboratory: a small mass "zero-transported" anywhere on the planet causes fountains of molten matter to erupt from the poles in association with a phenomenon called the "Wave," an energy front of great force but, generally speaking, short range. Something goes wrong, however, and in the course of pursuing their research, the scientists of Rainbow manage to unleash a Wave that not only is far more destructive than anything seen so far, but shows no signs of stopping within the polar regions.

With this catastrophe as a backdrop, the characters of *Far Rainbow* exhibit emotional complexities that match or surpass the best moments of the fiction analyzed thus far. Two characters constitute the main narrative foci: one the already familiar Leonid Gorbovsky, the other, a young technician named Robert Sklyarov. Robert is certainly the most complicated figure in the plot. His point of view dominates the first chapter, where we learn of his passion for the girl Tanya and of his weighty self-doubts. He is working with physicists on a laboratory planet with only a dim awareness of the reasoning behind his tasks. He is, in fact, one of the "little people of science," a somewhat shortsighted, pragmatic sort, according to the mysterious and more-than-human Camill.

An unpopular genius with strange powers of precognition, Camill has foreseen the disaster that befalls Rainbow, and he and Robert are the first on the planet to confront the Wave. Its effects are felt well before it appears above the horizon as a sparkling stripe across the sky, brighter than the sun. During the two-man evacuation of the research outpost, Camill is apparently crushed to death beneath some heavy equipment. When Robert returns by air to the main lab, however, Camill turns up via video to report on the Wave's progress, thus casting general doubt on Robert's veracity and humanity. Camill's resurrection remains unexplained until the story's end; the Strugatskys are fond of such teasing mysteries, which occur throughout their work.

As the Wave progresses, the scientific concerns of the planet's community continue to battle the human concerns. At one point, an apprehensive administrator begs the head zero-physicist, Lamondois, to make some attempt to stop the Wave before all means of supporting the population—crops, energy stations, etc.—are destroyed. Lamondois replies that "Rainbow is a physicist's planet, a laboratory," and that he intends to pursue his investigation of the Wave as long as possible. Not until the midpoint of the story does it become clear that all the arguments concerning the Wave are moot, since nothing *can* stop it.

The chapter in which this fact is discovered opens dramatically enough with the terse statement, "Robert saw it all happen." What follows is a chilling description of the approaching Wave, of the explosive failures of the mammoth energy-gulping machines sent out to slow its progress, and, in the foreground, of the details of the evacuation. The striking contrast between the matter-of-fact and even trivial minutiae of the latter with the overwhelming spector of disaster shows the authors at their stylistic best. Consider, for example, this passage:

> The vestibule was littered with pieces of wrapping paper and the parts of some apparatus. The door, made of shatterproof glass, was broken in half. Robert squeezed out sideways onto the porch and stopped. He watched the crammed, jammed pterocars rising up into the sky one after another....He saw Hassan and Carl, mouths open with exertion, trying to push their sarcophagus into the hatch of a helicopter and a man inside trying to help, and he saw the sarcophagus hit the man on his fingers time and time again. He saw Patrick, completely calm, sleepy Patrick, leaning against the rear light of the helicopter, looking intent and meditative. And turning his head, he saw the coal-black wall of the Wave, hiding the sky with a

velvet curtain, almost over his head. [Collier edition, 1980, p. 78]

Robert and his friend Patrick demonstrate a brand of heroism of which the Strugatskys obviously approve when they risk their lives to make sure the evacuation succeeds. But it is typical of the ambivalence with which the character of Robert is handled that in the next sequence he sacrifices a busload of children to the Wave in order to save his lover Tanya.

Meanwhile, at the equatorial Capital, the inevitable disaster has finally been acknowledged: the Wave rolling down from the North Pole and an identical one coming up from the South will be meeting at the equator in a matter of hours, obliterating all life on the planet. Everyone who can be found is being gathered to the Capital, where engineers are digging underground shelters in vain while the citizenry discusses the options open to it. The maelstrom of rumor makes it virtually impossible to distinguish between fact and fiction. In this setting, a public forum takes place where the arch-scientist Lamondois gives an impromptu speech firmly endorsing scientific values over moral ones. "Conversations on moral issues are always very difficult and unpleasant," he says with unconscious irony on his part. He further argues that the need to know transcends all other considerations. But before he can finish, he breaks down and confesses that he fears for his own life and his children's lives as well.

The question now at hand is who (or what) will safely leave the planet on Gorbovsky's interstellar freighter, which lies waiting in the Capital's port. Gorbovsky, who has thus far spent the novel lounging about sharing his sunny view of life with the locals, eventually takes the podium from Lamondois and gently informs the public that in actuality there is nothing left to discuss or decide: he, as Captain of the ship, has already given the order. The children on the planet, and *only* the children, will be saved. As for abstract philosophical considerations, Gorbovsky asserts, "In general, Comrade Lamondois expressed some interesting ideas. I would enjoy debating with him, but I must go." Why the children? "Our most valuable asset is our future," Gorbovsky responds. Once again a familiar Strugatsky theme expressed earlier in *Space Apprentice* and *Noon* is evoked by the Captain: our future is the children [p. 108].

The penultimate chapter that follows is short but painfully effective. The authors do not yield to the pathos and melodrama inherent in the situation. As it is, they restrict themselves to a simple description of the loading of the children onto the ship, while parents look on and while one artist or scientist after another petitions Gorbovsky to take along his personal creation. Gorbovsky finally permits these creators to place their material brain-children in a heap beside the hatch; no one seriously believes there will be room for any of them. He must also turn away a frantic and particularly selfish mother, who ultimately succeeds in sneaking aboard the ship, and talk a group of teenagers who desire a heroic martyrdom into boarding. There is also a tense, quietly dramatic incident as Robert Sklyarov appears with his Tanya and demands that she be taken aboard. Angry at Robert, she refuses before Gorbovsky can.

When the loading is finished, first Falkenstein, Gorbovsky's sullen first officer, then Dixon, the genial navigator, matter-of-factly insist on staying behind to make room for the children. Gorbovsky does not argue, but shoves the surprised schoolmaster on board the vessel, which Dixon has set on automatic pilot, and locks the hatch behind him, having elected, apparently some time before, to remain on Rainbow himself.

The final chapter is quiet—deathly quiet. The old companions from the starship say final good-byes as they head off to pass their last moments in different ways, Dixon driving off down the corridor between the two Waves, Mark Falkenstein heading off to the prairie with a female companion, Gorbovsky walking back toward the town in the loose company of others. Along the main street of the Capital, artists have set up an impromptu exhibition of their work, and in a patio cafe a young man performs music of his own composition. Hope has not completely died for some; a group of engineers yet continues to dig tunnels under the city, prompting Gorbovsky to observe how funny it is that "the most skeptical and logical men on the planet were hoping for a miracle...."

Gorbovsky finds himself a comfortable spot on the beach where he can relax until the end comes. Robert drifts by, cursing himself for his sins of that day. Gorbovsky consoles him with some comforting and forgiving words, then encourages him to spend his last minutes mending his ties with Tanya. He speaks with Camill, who reveals finally that he is the last survivor of an experiment that merged men with machines; Camill cannot die, and he faces the near prospect of complete isolation on a dead planet. Like the disastrous experimentation that caused the Wave, Camill is thus another example of the error

34

of subordinating the human to the starkly scientific. So is the last image of a small group of zero-transport test-pilots carrying a blind comrade, the victim of one such test, into the ocean and swimming away between the high black walls of the Wave. The injured man, playing a banjo, sings a song about hope in the face of adversity:

> When, like the dark waters,
> Calamity, terrible and bad,
> Came upon you
> You didn't bend your head,
> You looked into the sky
> And went on... [p. 131]

The characters in this novel, by and large, behave with a brand of heroism the Strugatskys clearly accept—a heroism not rooted in egoism or carelessness but born of necessity with an eye to the preservation of the future, in this case the children.

Far Rainbow demonstrates better than anything so far the Strugatskys' skill at producing vivid individual characters before a backdrop that expresses a broader purpose. The overarching message of this short novel concerns the danger inherent in pure scientific research pursued without thought for the moral consequences, a warning that looms large in our own time in the form of the Bomb. There is little to nothing here of the ideological polemics of the earlier novels. Yet somehow, even as a tragedy, *Far Rainbow* preserves the hope and humanism of the earlier works; indeed, it is a prime example of the aforementioned Marxist genre, "optimistic tragedy," which permits some esthetic leeway within the framework of utopian socialism. As the Strugatskys' career moved further into the decade of the sixties and their art continued to grow in complexity, such optimism would not come so readily.

III.

OF HISTORY AND HUMAN NATURE

All of the fiction considered so far has been set amid the ideal communism of the not-too-distant future. Dramatic conflict has been generated in this universe by ideological confrontations (in the nearest future only), by personal setbacks that probably serve as metaphors for the temporary obstacles standing in the way of Marxist goals, and by the consequences of unfettered scientific research. Historically, for a Soviet science fiction writer to bring into sharper focus the differences between communism and other ideologies, he was until recently forced by the optimistic assumptions of the Party line to move off the planet, to others where history's dialectic is not so near its consummation; one could not depict a future Earth that has failed to become a world socialist state.

According to the official Soviet version of Marx—which some Western Marxist scholars claim was a distortion of Marx's actual ideas—all cultures pass through a series of well-marked political and economic phases. The first, the primitive mode, is the preliterate tribal form of communism, in which a community holds all its property in common. In the next phase, the "Ancient" in the West and the "Asiatic" in the East, an absolute emperor or despot rises to the apex of a society, the foundation of which is slave labor. This mode evolves into a decentralized feudalism, dominated by petty fiefdoms, a land-based agricultural economy, and serf labor. Feudalism is inevitably displaced by capitalism, either peacefully as in Great Britain in 1688 or violently as in the France of 1789. Under the capitalist mode the revolution continues, as capitalists consolidate their power in fewer and fewer hands until they are eventually outnumbered by the alienated and disenfranchised working classes. The latter rise up, wrest power from the capitalists, and set society on the road to utopia. If for some reason, however, the ultimate revolution of labor is postponed, capitalism degenerates into fascism, with its dictatorship of the bourgeoisie, its concentration of power in a narrow elite, and its maintenance of rule through domestic terrorism and military force. Fascism is considered a historical anomaly, an accident, a disorder caused by the derailment of the normal, inevitable course of history.

In common with other utopian literatures, Russian science fiction has a long tradition of using foreign and alien settings as stages for philosophical fables. In the 1920s, for instance, during the first Marxian invasion of the genre outlined above, many other worlds became host to the horrors of capitalism. Arkady and Boris Strugatsky were thus on solid ground when they left their Marxian Earth behind to investigate human societies on less fortunate planets.

Popytka k begstvu (published in English as *Escape Attempt*; Macmillan, 1982) first appeared in 1962, while the Strugatskys were still finishing up the utopian cycle discussed in the last chapter. In this novella, travelers from the communist Earth of the future visit a planet inhabited by human beings in the feudal stage of civilization. Joining the starfarers in their disgust at the violent abuses of this system is a comrade who claims to be a specialist in twentieth-century history. He provides periodic comparisons between the feudalism at hand and the capitalism of his own era of expertise. In addition, the planet of the story has been visited at one time by the Wanderers, an ancient star-hopping race that receives mention in a number of Strugatsky fictions, who have left behind several puzzling artifacts. Eventually, one of the future Earthmen, unable to deal with the realities of feudalism, suffers a breakdown, after which the supposed historian reveals himself to be a Soviet soldier from World War II, who had reached Earth's utopian future simply by wishing it. After all he has witnessed, he opts to return to the war to risk his life, that the communist future may be realized.

When this story was re-published in 1965, it was joined to a novel that examines a different stage of history and one much closer to home: *Khishchnye veshchi veka*, which translates as *Predatory Things of Our Times* but which appeared in English as *The Final Circle of Paradise*. It brings Ivan Zhilin, the good-natured ship engineer of *Space Apprentice*, back to his beloved Earth in an unusual role; he is a secret agent masquerading as a tourist in a city-state that is one of the last refuges of decadent capitalism. A resort area, it is a place of superficial affluence that thinly conceals the boredom and spiritual malaise of the populace. To fill their empty lives and empty hours, the natives and tourists both seek out the many cheap thrills the city offers, such as the abandoned subway where people pay to experience a life-and-death chase with a crazed robot. All values have been reduced to the service of hedonism, including those of science and technology. Much of the food is artificial, like the well-groomed appearance of the natives. Even stranger and more sinister is the popularity of the "shivers," a form of mass hysteria induced by the direct electronic stimulation of the pleasure centers of the brain. Along similar lines, but more deadly in its effects, is "slug," a more private blend of electronic and chemical stimulation that has the unfortunate side-effect of slowly destroying its users, much like heroin.

Zhilin's job is to root out the causes and, if possible, the people behind the degeneracy of this society. In the process, he must track down and attempt to communicate with the two agents who preceded him, Peck and Rimeyer. Following several mysterious episodes, he finally discovers that Peck has become one of the major dealers in "slug," and that Rimeyer is himself hopelessly addicted to it. Out of a sort of scientific curiosity, and to better understand what he is dealing with, Zhilin even tries slug himself. He finds it a potent escape indeed, but is not converted to it. It does, however, help him reach the surprising conclusion that no particular set of individuals is responsible for the spiritual decline of this or any other culture: the responsibility lies with all people and the unfortunately all-too-human blend of inventiveness and self-centered sensuality. Ironically, his direct superiors refuse to accept his findings, insisting that "if there is a crime, there must be a criminal."

Decadence is catching because human beings are weak. And human weakness in this novel leads to consequences a good deal more serious than the petty "philistinism" of the earlier works, consequences that approach something resembling evil. Added to the boredom, materialism, selfishness, hedonism, artificiality, philosophical paucity, and scientific charlatanism criticized within the narrative are frequent references to gangsterism and fascism. Two elusive texts mentioned in the course of the story are, tellingly, the *History of Fascism* and the *Sociology of Decaying Economic Structures*. In this society, abundance and affluence have become ends in themselves instead of becoming the means to a better world.

At one point late in the narrative, Zhilin engages in a dialectical exchange with a Rimeyer of his imagination concerning the means and ends of history. Zhilin argues that the task of human beings is to interreact in order to produce genuine social progress. Zhilin's

Rimeyer insists in return that progress, in the form of science and technology, has produced slug, which can provide every individual a personal paradise without pain or struggle, work or sacrifice. Slug fulfills the *illusion* of material and spiritual well-being. That, says the imaginary Rimeyer, and not the socialist utopia, may be the logical end of history.

Zhilin refuses to accept Rimeyer's vision of the future, even as he recognizes, fearfully, the charm it could hold for too many people. But although he lays the blame for the evils of society at the feet of Everyman, he does not view humankind as inherently bad. The key to salvation, for Zhilin, is education. When he opposes his superiors in their interpretation of the local situation, he opposes as well their solution: isolating the city from the rest of the world and cleaning it up by force. He wants to re-train the minds of the people, "to return to people their souls which had been devoured by affluence, and to teach each one to think of world problems in the same way as his own personal ones" (DAW, 1976; p. 169-170). He decides to remain in the Country of the Boob, if nothing else to save a boy he has befriended there, a boy horrified by his surroundings, and the child's fellows. Again, the future lies in the children.

As noted in the Introduction, several Soviet critics found this work flawed on ideological grounds; they maintained, somewhat carpingly, that the Country of the Boob was not identified, nor its economic foundation precisely enough defined. The implication seemed to be that such a pocket of decadent capitalism had no place in the ideal Marxist future Earth, even though in the context of the Strugatskys' early work it should have been clear that this enclave, like the corrupt Bamberga of *Space Apprentice*, is supposed to be a relic of a passing era. Perhaps these ideological critics, like Zhilin's stubborn colleagues Oscar and Matya, expected a clear-cut criminal or clique of gangsters, economically oppressing the people, who could be blamed for the sorry state of society and be excised. Instead, the novel offers the vision of a humanity only too willing to be corrupted by abundance and affluence, and by mere pleasure.

Of the three thematically important dialogues that take place at the novel's end (the two already mentioned being those between Zhilin and the imagined Rimeyer and between Zhilin and his fellow agents), one in particular dramatizes the difficulty of Zhilin's desperate hope to improve the state of humanity. In a well-appointed cafe, he runs into a revolutionary, apparently African, who has come to the Country of the

Boob in pursuit of arms and other support for his cause. Despite all his talk of liberating his poor and oppressed folk from a dictatorial regime, however, he is no Marxist. He overtly admires the plenty he sees around him, and argues that such material abundance is alone worth fighting for, over and above such abstracts as democracy. Zhilin's reply is that the great revolutionaries did not say "now you are free—enjoy yourselves," but "now you are free—work." The third-worlder immediately calls Zhilin a Marxist and automatically reaches for his pistol.

If the presentation of the message is somewhat unorthodox, there can be no doubt that the message itself—that progress is rooted not in mere material abundance and a devotion to pleasure, but in more broadly humanistic values—is essentially Marxist, in the best sense of the word. That the Strugatskys' ideological critics could not recognize as much can only be attributed to a certain conservative contrariness or ossified thinking on their part.

If the ideological charges ring false, one *can* demonstrate a certain lack of artistic focus in the novel. While the Strugatskys do achieve an ominous sense of mystery throughout the first three-quarters of the book—here as elsewhere they enjoy teasing the reader with unsolved riddles—at one point there are so many loose threads in the plot that it risks unraveling. At the same time, the blanket condemnation of all the sins of decadence casts so wide that a number of the intended interrelationships—for instance, between leisure, gangsterism, and scientific charlatanism—remain so vague they must be taken on faith. Darko Suvin has noted that the novel owes something to the hard-boiled detective school best exemplified by Raymond Chandler: the Chandleresque first-person narrative, for instance, as well as the sinister and seamy activities of the plot and the morally ambiguous characters. Zhilin, however, is anything but hard-boiled, a stance which requires a large measure of cynicism about the perfectability of human society. It is difficult to mix the twisted morality of such fiction with the positivist dialectics of Marx, and Zhilin is definitely a mild-mannered Marxist. The authors succeed in spots, but on the whole the work is not one of their best.

The most that can be said of *The Final Circle of Paradise*, from the perspective of the nineties, is that it foreshadows in surprising ways the American "cyberpunk" movement of the mid-eighties. As in cyberpunk, a hard-boiled style depicts a glitzy if corrupt society dominated by powerful monied institutions and given over to drugs, electronic stimulation of the nervous system, and mass media manipulation. The critique of capitalism is often only implied in the work of writers like Gibson, Sterling, and Shirley, where the driving purpose of everyone from the multinational corporation to the street pusher is wealth and the pleasure it can buy, to the moral degradation of all. This message is explicit in *The Final Circle of Paradise*.

Such lack of subtlety no longer pleases the sophisticated Western taste, though it may have been more acceptable when the novel first appeared; one is reminded of the overt, self-assured philosophizing of, say, a Robert Heinlein. Apparently, however, it was too subtle for the aforementioned Soviet critics seeking a clear confirmation of the Party's assessment of historical inevitability. Despite its humanely anti-capitalist stance, this novel unleashed the half decade of ideological controversy concerning the brothers' work outlined in the Introduction.

The novel that *is* considered their best by many critics of East and West is the one that appeared just before *Paradise*, in 1964. It too concerns the issue of history and human nature; indeed, it is probably the Strugatskys' master work on this subject. *Trudno byt' bogom*, which was translated literally as *Hard To Be a God* when it appeared in English in 1973, became the most popular work of the Strugatsky brothers in the Soviet Union and for a while in the sixties the most popular work of science fiction by any author. Much of the novel's success derives from its blending a swashbuckling plot and characters with much serious and even pessimistic dialectical philosophizing.

The hero, known in the main text as Don Rumata, is a member of a team from the Institute of Experimental History, sent from an advanced, communist Earth to study the human life of an alien planet. Like the world of *Escape Attempt*, this planet is passing through the feudal stage of history. Unfortunately, it is also defying the logic of Marx by degenerating further, into fascism, without having passed first through the capitalist phase. Masquerading as nobles (thus the title "Don"), Rumata and his colleagues in the feudal land of Arkanar find themselves forced to deal with a petty bourgeois consolidation of power under the Stormtrooper-like Gray Soldiers and their leader Don Reba. A former government official, Reba, though notable chiefly for his mediocrity, nonetheless wields tremendous powers of terror. His major support among the populace comes from the rising class of shopkeepers, who are suspicious of the old intelligentsia and aristocracy and are out to destroy both. They are aided in this endeavor by the Church, particularly the militant monks of the Holy Order, and ultimately by the night army of the underworld bandit leader Waga Koleso. Here we have the classic triumvirate of Marxist arch-villains—petty bourgeois, cleric, and gangster—uniting to squelch the seeds of the enlightenment that would facilitate the transition from feudalism through capitalism to the communist world state, "a society freed of all class distinctions and the oppression of man," in Rumata's words.

Rumata and his comrades from the Institute of Experimental History are bound by the Institute's code to avoid direct intervention in the affairs of the planet and are forbidden by the enlightened ethics of Earth from killing another human being. Nevertheless, Rumata feels compelled to do whatever he can to prevent the injustices he sees around him and to help save this society from the political cancer that infects it. He finds himself losing the necessary detachment of an outside investigator, primarily because he has grown to love his adopted land and a native woman, Kyra. It is the conflict between the enlightened Earthman and the passionate Arkanarian in Rumata that gives him his depth and the story its complexity; Rumata is not just another sword-wielder in the mode of heroic fantasy.

This tension in Rumata's character is central to the plot of the novel, as evidenced by various crises in the narrative that focus on Rumata's confrontations with enemies and, simultaneously, with his own increasing impulses toward violence. The first such episode takes place near the beginning of Chapter Three, when Rumata, having just discovered he has been robbed, spots a pair of Gray Soldiers, also known as Sturmoviki, sneering at him. Rumata experiences a double reaction: "As far as the collaborator and member of the Institute of Experimental History was concerned, they could simply go to Hell—but the noble don flew into a rage. For a moment he lost control" (DAW, 1974; p. 67). He approaches the soldiers as if to attack, and after they flee to the safety of a tavern he realizes he would have killed them had they not. He is stunned by this realization and can rationalize his behavior only on the grounds that "I am a human being, in spite of everything, so there must be animal in me as well."

The next such moment of epiphany comes in Chapter Four, after Rumata spends a night drinking with a hearty but hedonistic native friend, one Baron Pampa. Only the next morning does he remember brawling in taverns and bursting into the house of his lover Kyra with violation on his mind. Though he goes through a ritual of cleansing himself that morning before humbling himself in front of Kyra, his humanity appears to have suffered a permanent change. A chapter later, after he haughtily insults a Sturmovik guard, he analyzes this change: he has actually become this "lout of noble birth" named Don Rumata; he now truly despises his enemies and his social inferiors, this "wonderful creature called 'man'."

Anton, the Earthman behind the mask of Rumata, is degenerating in response to his environment. Feudal Arkanar has no place for an enlightened individual, as Anton-Rumata recognizes with increasing bitterness over the course of the narrative. And the problem of this society and its Gray Horde has no simple solution. At one point early in the novel, Rumata fantasizes somewhat to his own disgust about massacring Reba and his army. In his imagination, however, chaos follows: Waga Koleso's bandits overrun the unprotected country, as do the barbarians from the mountains; the terrified citizenry is forced to flee to the wilderness to starve or be slaughtered, while the nobles butcher each other in a struggle for power. Rumata is not far from the actual truth of a later event, the Night of Long Knives. During this incident, reminiscent of the bloodiest episodes of Nazism, Don Reba turns the Gray Soldiers loose on the capital city. Joined by Koleso's nocturnal army, they slaughter all those targeted by Reba's petty bourgeois movement, including a number of the bourgeoisie themselves. The Sturmoviki, in turn, are massacred and supplanted by the mounted monks of the Holy Order, who set the opportunistic Reba up as nominal dictator while retaining considerable power.

In the wake of this coup, Rumata continues to acknowledge the evil residing in all feasible social alternatives. In a discussion in Chapter Eight with a fugitive intellectual, Doctor Budach, Rumata asks the other's opinion regarding what God should do to make the best world for human beings. When the doctor suggests providing all people the necessities of life, Rumata replies in God's place that the strong would continue to take from the weak. When the doctor suggests that cruel rulers be enlightened, Rumata points out that enlightened rulers would be replaced by crueler, and thus stronger men. The picture Rumata ends up composing of mankind is one in which the strong incessantly oppress the weak, in which the satisfaction of all needs produces either greed or apathy, and in which the only certain route to human happiness appears to be to "'wipe this mankind off the face of the Earth and create another in its place.'"

The point is driven home further in the following chapter, while Rumata converses with the rebel leader Arata. The latter is an admirable if tragic figure, partly blinded and crippled by the violent efforts of his past. He has led one group of slaves or serfs after another to revolt, only to see them either turn on each other, resume the ways of slaves, or replace their oppressors as oppressors themselves. As Rumata silently observes, "You don't know that your enemy is not to be found beyond the ranks of your own soldiers, but rather within themselves" [p. 192]. All alternatives to the ugly, violent society of Arkanar seem to be negated by the nature of its humankind.

Still, in characteristic Strugatsky fashion, a glimmer of hope remains. Even in Arkanar mankind is not inherently evil, merely innately prone to evil. Rumata observes as much after a few moments of tender interaction with the ten-year-old prince of Arkanar. This child, along with the other children he has met in the country, "showed absolutely no trace of meanness." Yet these children, Rumata muses, "were the ones who would later develop bestiality, ignorance, and blind submission to the authorities" [p. 130]. As he looks out over the city covered by night, he reminds himself that these people "were not yet human beings in the current sense of the word, but rather preliminary stages, blocks of raw iron ore out of which the bloody centuries of history would eventually forge proud and free men" [p. 131].

The power of the environment to shape or destroy the human spirit is demonstrated most dramatically in the novel's climax. When a detachment of the vicious monks of the Holy Order tries to injure Rumata indirectly by attacking the home of his beloved Kyra, he leaps to her defense. She ends up being killed by a crossbow, however, and the last we see of Rumata on the planet he is waiting, a sword in each hand and bloody revenge in his thoughts, for the monks to break through the door. A victim of his love for Kyra and his passionate involvement in his adopted land, he has given himself up wholly to the violence of this world and the more barbarian impulses of his humanity.

An interesting, if to some mystifying, perspective on the events of the main narrative is provided by a Prologue and Epilogue that frame it. Both take place in the Russian countryside of the future utopian Earth and feature Anton—the Don Rumata of Arkanar—and his friends Pashka (Don Hug on the other planet) and Anka. In the Prologue they are children enjoying a pastoral afternoon. Following some swashbuckling play, the games turn more serious when Anton accepts the girl Anka's dare to shoot Pashka's hat off his head with a crossbow, William Tell style. Though Anton purposely aims too high, the fact that he shoots at all, taking an unnecessary risk with human life, sours the afternoon. Anton finally turns his back on his companions to explore an abandoned one-way road, what he calls an "anisotropic" road. As the children row home that evening, Anton tells the others that at the end of the road he found a collapsed bridge and the old skeleton of a Nazi soldier chained to a machine gun.

After the sojourn on Arkanar, the three are reunited in the short Epilogue, where Pashka reveals to Anka that Anton had suffered a breakdown (somewhat like the Earthman in *Escape Attempt*) and hideously massacred the monks at his last stand. The Institute of Experimental History had immediately taken Anton off the planet and returned him to the Russian woods for a long, gradual convalescence. While Anka waits for Anton to appear, Pashka reminds her of the occasion when Anton walked the one-way road and discovered the Nazi skeleton. Pashka further muses: "Maybe there's some connection somewhere...the road was anisotropic—just as history is. *There is no way back*. And he went right ahead anyway. And met up with a chained skeleton" [p. 204]. Anka does not see the significance of the event, however, about which even Pashka is uncertain.

Their confusion was shared by some Soviet critics who found this frame tale vague or at worst another example of mysticism. But it can be read as a metaphor for the Rumata plot and its moral. As Pashka notes, the road that Anton explored was "one-way," like history. Anton, therefore, walked backwards down the road of history until he met with a relic of humanity's barbarism—a skeleton, man's basic structure, bound to an artifact of war. That the skeleton is dressed in a Nazi uniform is a reminder, especially to us in the twentieth century, that the darker side of human nature and the vicious political accidents it can provoke are matters of recent memory. Anton demonstrates the corollary to this moral: that it is virtually impossible to deal with such barbarism without losing one's own hard-earned civilization. The price paid out of one's humanity may be recoverable, however; in the parable, Anton did come back, after all.

The qualified pessimism of this novel is surprising considering it comes so close upon the conclusion of the utopian first stage of the Strugatskys' career. The work gets away with this revolution in tone largely because it is so entertaining; its disturbing message comes with fast action and heroic, if still fallibly human, characters. It manages to be philosophically provocative without falling prey to preachiness.

Only one other work of the Strugatsky brothers deals so seriously and directly with the problem of history and human nature, the 1971 novel *Obitaemyi ostrov*—literally translated, *The Inhabited Is-*

land. Published in English as *Prisoners of Power*, it contains a situation somewhat akin to that of the shorter *Hard To Be a God*: an Earthman from the far future has crashed on a planet inhabited by apparent humans. Coming from a peaceful, socialist Earth, the innocent Maxim Kammerer is initially confused and distressed by the world of violence he encounters. The planet is just recovering from a devastating nuclear war. The countryside crawls with robot military machinery and assorted human and animal mutations, and hostilities continue much in Cold War fashion, with border skirmishes and paramilitary rule in Maxim's new home, the Land of the All-Powerful Creators. Again the chief villain is fascism, kept in place here by the ruthless Fighting Legion. This highly disciplined army has as its primary task the eradication of a minority segment of the population known as "degens" (from "degenerates"). They can be identified by the severe pains they suffer while the rest of the populace is caught up in paroxysms of patriotism. Only much later does Maxim discover that the ruling All-Powerful Creators are controlling the masses through periodic strikes of mind-affecting radiation; it is this that causes the blind devotion of the majority and the blinding pains of the "degens."

Maxim's eyes open only gradually to the realities of life on this world, and during the course of his education he commits himself, Candide-like, to one course of action after another. While still a total *naif*, a "Robinson Crusoe" on the "inhabited island" of the book's Russian title, he befriends a legionnaire, Guy Gaal, and his family and ends up joining the Legion himself. What follows is a long critical look at the abuses of fascism: the unquestioned acceptance of authority, the cruelty, the violence, the bigotry, the inhumanity. Maxim remains with the Legion for an unrealistically long time, not because it is consonant with his character, but because the authors have a point to make. Only when ordered to execute a group of degens he has come to know and respect does he abandon some of his naïveté, and with it, the Legion.

We next see him joining the degen underground. He overcomes their natural suspicion of him in part through a demonstration of his more-than-human powers; by this point in the narrative it has become clear that the Earthman of the future is further along the scale of evolution than that of today. For one thing, Maxim has been able to recover fully from six gunshots delivered to vital organs during his desertion of the Legion. He can also see in the dark, perceive radiation outside the visible range, and perform prodigious feats of strength. These talents serve him well as he joins the degen terrorists in their effort to blow up radiation towers. Unfortunately, he finds many members of the underground short-sighted, self-aggrandizing, and power-hungry, reminiscent of the experience of the rebel leader Arata in *Hard To Be a God*. Despite his commitment to their cause, he anguishes over the waste of human life and intelligence while reminding himself that such "miserable, stupid, evil people" must be expected from such a "miserable, stupid, evil world."

Maxim is finally captured and held prisoner for his terrorist activity. Taking advantage of his superpowers and his increasing knowledge about this world, he escapes to the borderlands in search of an ally in his fight against the All-Powerful Creators. Instead, he finds the country surrounded by communities of weak, provincial, and apathetic mutants, bloodthirsty barbarians, and equally vicious foreign states. He ultimately makes a heroic, single-handed effort to destroy the central radiation generator in the capital, and thus the power of the Creators, and succeeds. The Land of the All-Powerful Creators pitches into chaos and depression.

It is not until this point near the novel's end that Maxim meets Strannik, who has been a sinister figure throughout the narrative, one of the more highly placed All-Powerful Creators who has taken a particular interest in tracking Maxim down. It turns out, when they finally encounter one another, that even Maxim's triumph was born of naïveté; Strannik is himself an Earthman, part of an administration—perhaps identical to the one in *Hard To Be a God*—charged with intervening in the planet's history in order to get it on the proper road to progress. Strannik explains that the radiation was merely a way of keeping the population under control until a solution to the real problems of this world could be found. Maxim commits himself as well to the planet's progress, vowing to practice anything from economics to submarine warfare providing the central radiation generator not be rebuilt. He is determined that the people at least have some free choice in regards to their future.

We are told more than once in the novel that the society of this world has "swerved from the course of history," to use the words of Vepr, a leader of the degen underground. What is quite significant is that Vepr, who seems reliable, blames the government's control of the masses, via the radiation, for preventing them from recognizing their political and economic oppression, a necessary step in the natural Marxist process of revolution/evolution. Strannik, therefore, is directly if only partly responsible for the fascist foundations of the society, even though his goal is to promote the communist consummation of history. There may well be a parallel here between Strannik's use of fascist methods toward communist ends and Stalin's; the super-patriotism, militarism, and domestic terrorism practiced by the Fighting Legion have nearly as much in common with Stalinism as with the more obvious Nazism. By rejecting Strannik's methods, Maxim is insisting that the means must match the humanity of the end.

Maxim has in no way remained above reproach, however. Like Anton-Rumata in the earlier novel, he too has his soul soiled by contact with barbarism. He does not even have Rumata's guilty conscience. Early in the book, for instance, he is attacked by a group of men while walking a city street at night. Using his powers, he dilates his psychological time and kills six of them within seconds. When it occurs to him afterward that these were actually human beings, he "sensed that he had lost something fine and pure, a part of his soul, and he realized that the old Maxim had disappeared forever" [Collier, 1978; p. 44]. While he avoids being completely brutalized as a legionnaire, he does not quail at slaughtering the enemy during his period as a terrorist. Initially gentle in his innocence, Maxim grows steadily fiercer the wiser he becomes to the planet. Late in the book, during a tremendous massacre induced by the All-Powerful Creators and their Fighting Legion, Maxim's humanity reaches a major crisis. He decides he will stop the battle by bodily dragging all the legionnaires from their tanks. As he contemplates the violent force on his part that this task will require, he realizes that "that was precisely what he wanted now. Never before had he craved the feel of human flesh beneath his fingers" [p. 243].

Finally, when he sets the bomb in the medical center that secretly houses the central radiation generator, a bomb that will take with it several dozen human beings, strangers and acquaintances alike, Maxim justifies his act on the grounds that "[t]he place is a nest, a snake's nest, full of the most choice trash, trash collected with great care, gathered here for the express purpose of converting into more trash all those within reach of the emitters' sorcery. All of them are enemies of the people, and not one of them would hesitate for a moment to shoot, betray, or crucify me...and all my friends" [p. 277]. Ironically, this quarter of the novel—each of which is named to reflect the continuing development of the hero—bears the title "Earthling." Though his goals are honorable—like, we presume, Strannik's—he too has adopted, or been infected by, the brutality and the restricted conscience of the world that surrounds him, a world resembling nothing so much as the Cold War Earth.

As has already been hinted, Maxim's character is not particularly consistent, nor is he as complex a figure as the hero of *Hard To Be a God*. *Prisoners of Power* is more fabulous, coming in the wake of the fantastic mode with which the authors experimented in the latter half of the sixties (see Chapter 3 below). Unlike the fantasies, however, it deals specifically with the subject of history and human nature, justifying comparison with *Hard To Be a God*.

The last word on this subject so far appears in the 1976 novelette "Paren' iz preispodnei" ("The Guy from Hell"). It too falls back on the now almost formulaic situation of Earthly intervention in a nonterrestrial culture, with elements of all the other works discussed in this chapter. The main diffference is that this time the title character, Corporal Gahg, is an extraterrestrial from a violent planet removed to a utopian Earth, where he learns to be an advanced, peace-loving human being, thus reversing the course taken by Anton and Maxim. Like them, however, he is subject to the influence of his immediate environment, here with happier results, reaffirming the authors' thesis on this point.

Of all the stories on this topic, *Hard To Be a God* would probably interest the most readers, having the right balance of appealing characters, an entertaining plot, and a convincing approach to its theme. *Prisoners of Power* would come in second, only because it requires more patience and objectivity on the reader's part; the story is longer and less realistic, the protagonist a bit more resistant to reader identification.

The relative darkness of these two novels may obscure the authors' persistent assumption that human progress, at least in these works, is still inevitable, an assumption that carries over from the decidedly brighter first phase of their career. After all, the cultures on the alien worlds of these fictions copy Earth itself in earlier stages of history—the Dark Ages in *Hard To Be a God*, the Cold War in *Prisoners of Power*. The Earthmen of the future represent more advanced forms of humanity, Anton with his wisdom, ethics, and various skills, Maxim with his superhuman powers. Both presumably evolved from the humankind we know, that recognizable in the brutal, miserable, shortsighted creatures who inhabit the worlds of the novels. Anton, Maxim, and the other emissaries from Earth come from classless, Marxian utopias where all the problems they confront on their adopted planets have long since ceased to exist. Ultimately, the reader must assume, these planets will also go the way of Earth. The other side of this coin is that humanity's less humane tendencies never disappear completely; even the super-evolved Maxim falls prey to them. The human animal remains the same; only education and environment make any difference, and especially the latter.

Though *Prisoners of Power* and "The Guy from Hell" were the last works of the Strugatskys rooted specifically in the problem of meshing the Soviet theory of historical progression with the empirical realities of human weakness, elements of this dialectic do appear elsewhere. The increasing irresolution and pessimism of later pieces suggest that the Strugatskys have not yet solved the question to their satisfaction. It is a tribute to their artistic and philosophical integrity that, despite the readiness of the simple answers of which they availed themselves in their early career, they have concluded by leaving the discussion open.

IV.

FANTASY AND SATIRE

Following the success of *Hard To Be a God* and the controversies of *The Final Circle of Paradise*, the Strugatskys' fiction veered away from political economics. The period 1965-1968 saw four long works produced that abandon realistic and futuristic modes to tread the boundary of fantasy and satire. Though these also touch on the previously handled themes of human institutions, human nature, and the applications of science, they do so in a whimsical and even surreal fashion.

A number of reasons could be offered for this change in strategy. As noted in Chapter I, Russian literary history offers ample examples of writers using the fantastic and satirical, often in combination, and most often when addressing controversial political and social questions. In tsarist Russia, both supporters and detractors of the system utilized fantasy and satire; opponents hoped in so doing to avoid the risks involved in direct challenges to the official line.

It is tempting for Western critics to see the Strugatsky brothers' movement away from the realism of their early work as a similar attempt to avoid official disapproval. Arguing against that view is the fact that these fictions were, if anything, more blunt in their attacks on bureaucratic conservatism and popular apathy than anything they had written before. Except for the first of them, it was these very fantasies that deepened the critical and ideological controversy over their work that began with *The Final Circle of Paradise*.

A broader possibility is suggested by István Csicery-Ronay, Jr., who observes, in an article cited in Chapter I, that the Strugatskys' science fiction, and Soviet science fantasy in general, is never far from the Russian fairy tale paradigm outlined in Vladimir Propp's classic study, *The Morphology of the Folk-Tale*. Propp's scheme offers a simple folk hero who leaves home to retrieve a loss, right a wrong, or protect a loved one; in the course of his quest, he (or sometimes she)

53

must undergo various ordeals, outwit a false hero or defeat a villain, and return home with magic aid, to a marriage and a throne. As part of its formal endorsement of the folk arts, revolutionary Leninism embraced the Russian fairy tale, with its emphasis on the defeat of powerful opponents and the triumph of the common man (or woman), as a model for socialist literature.

If in their early utopian science fiction the Strugatskys managed to carry over some of this fairy tale idealism, their fantasies of the late sixties partake somewhat more of the absurdism of Nikolai Gogol and Franz Kafka, or the deflating, if officially sanctioned, satire of Ilf and Petrov and the Soviet Magazine *Krokodil*. The Strugatskys' simple heroes are less likely to overcome enemies and marry princesses than they are to find themselves, anti-heroically, at the mercy of incomprehensible and even alien forces beyond their control.

Of all of these fantasies, the closest to traditional Russian fairy tale motifs and the most congenial was the first published, *Ponedel'nik nachinaetsia v subbotu*—in English, *Monday Begins on Saturday*. This 1965 novel posits a research facility far in the mystical Russian North, the Scientific Research Institute for Thaumaturgy and Spellcraft, where the techniques of modern science and ancient magic freely blend. Alexander Privalov, a vacationing computer programmer, finds himself drafted by a couple of its researchers; almost immediately he comes up against a series of bizarre phenomena—strange voices coming out of a mirror, a hut kept by a hag that gets up on hen's legs in the middle of the night, a singing, tale-telling cat tied to an oak in which a mermaid sits, and so on—all familiar to those acquainted with the rich canon of Russian folklore. Also recognizable would be the talking pike who grants wishes; characteristic of the modern, mundane Privalov is his first thought on discovering the fish's talents: having the pike service his car.

The mixture of the modern and the mystical remains a recurring motif throughout the book. Quasi-rational explanations are offered for nearly all the appurtenances of magic. When Privalov discovers a magic wand under a piece of furniture, for instance, a figure in a gray suit appears and warns him against using it without the proper scientific background and technical training. Similarly, a sofa with mysterious properties turns out to be a transistorized "translator" with an invisible on-off switch in its springs. Encantations are treated like scientific formulae. The entire book abounds with such touches; the fusion and confusion of technology and magic is its longest running joke.

54

Whimsy, with a hint of satire, motivates other motifs in the book. For example, the various departments of the research center have absurd titles that match their objectives: Linear Happiness, Meaning of Life, Defensive Magic, Universal Transformations, and so on. Some aspects of the Institute and its work remind one of the tour of the Academy in the Third Book of *Gulliver's Travels*. The ultimate scientific charlatan is one Ambrosi Vibegallo, head of the Department of Absolute Knowledge. Vibegallo is, for one thing, a humorous archetype of the inefficient administrator; everyone under his authority wastes time by taking end-to-end vacations or on projects like dividing zero into zero. Vibegallo is also a bad scientist, prone to grandstanding for the media and creating useless or harmful experiments. When we see him, he is engaged in hatching the ideal man, working up to him in stages such as "Man, unsatisfied stomachwise." This particular model is the consummate consumer, who swallows tons of offal in Vibegallo's demonstration of the axiom that happiness comes from the satisfaction of the grossest physical wants. After the model consumer explodes in a shower of filth, Vibegallo conjures up the next stage of perfected humanity, the "superegocentrist." This humanoid not only swallows everything material in the vicinity but threatens, like a black hole, to warp time and space around itself before being destroyed.

The authors are not everywhere so unsympathetic to these practitioners of scientific wizardry, however. In one long serious passage, Privalov notes the dedication of most of the men at the Institute, men "who couldn't stand any kind of Sunday, because they were bored on Sunday. They were magi, Men with a capital M, and their motto was 'Monday begins on Saturday'" [DAW, 1977; p. 116]. Here, curiously, Privalov praises the very pursuits—the search for human happiness, absolute knowledge, and the meaning of life—treated humorously elsewhere, and in terms that suggest the authors' approval of his stance. This earnest, laudatory moment seems out of place in the middle of this otherwise playful narrative, but then the novel as a whole is a grab bag of somewhat random effects, some more successful than others.

One of the best sequences is a take-off on time travel that turns into a satire of the entire science fiction genre. Privalov volunteers to board an experimental time machine constructed along the lines of an automobile—somewhat anticipating the DeLorean of *Back to the Future*, except that this vehicle turns out to have clutch problems. Another drawback is that it can only visit *fictional* futures, those depicted in the science fiction of East and West.

Privalov's journey does in fact go back to find the future, beginning in classical times with two Grecian figures engaged in interminable Platonic dialogue about the utopian state. The future evolves into a medieval utopia in which the buildings change while the dialogue remains the same. Finally, utopian literature enters the nineteenth century, with a concomitant appearance of the industrial revolution, ubiquitous machinery, and crowds of translucent and partially dressed—because only superficially described—people.

As the twentieth-century future dawns, Privalov finds himself on a moving sidewalk—a significant detail when one recalls the symbolic importance of such in the utopian *Noon*. The first Soviet period of science fiction is marked by men in union suits marching and singing to Marxist hymns, followed by space travelers leaving *en masse* to carry the revolution to the stars while their women go into deep freeze to wait for them, surrounded by waving fields of wheat. A dialogue between two boys full of Gernsbackian pulp SF terminology ("I found out how to apply nonwearing tires here, made of polystructural fibers with denatured amino-bonds and incomplete oxygen groups.") proves to concern nothing more sophisticated than the bicycle.

At one point, a gray wall suddenly appears and is promptly identified as the Iron Curtain. On Privalov's side of it, people continue interminable educational sessions on everything from rocketry to music, while on the western side interminable war rages. Finally venturing through the wall, he finds himself surrounded by noisy violence.

> All five of my senses were instantly traumatized. I saw a good-looking blond with an indecent tattoo between her shoulder blades, all nakedness and long legs, firing two automatics into an ugly brunette, who showered red drops with each shot. I heard the thunder of explosions and the soul-rending cries of monsters. I smelled the indescribable stench of rotting and burned nonprotein flesh. The searing wind of a proximate nuclear explosion burned my face and I felt on my tongue the repulsive taste of pulverized protoplasm scattered through the atmosphere. [DAW, 1977; p. 166].

He returns in haste to the east of the wall and leaps ahead, only to find in front of him, to his groaning disappointment, the same Pantheon-Refrigerator where the women of Soviet SF wait frozen for their spacefaring men.

> A rusty spaceship of spherical shape was descending from the sky. There was no one around; wheat fields waved. The sphere landed and the erstwhile pilot in blue came out. The girl in pink appeared at the door of the Pantheon. She was covered by the red spots of bedsores. They ran toward each other and clasped hands. I turned away, feeling ill at ease. The blue pilot and the pink girl started a dreary dialogue. [p. 166].

After one last look at the West, which shows him a landscape of devastation, medieval institutions, and hostile aliens, Privalov's clutch gives out altogether, and he finds himself back in his present. The whole is a wonderful send-up of the tradition in which the Strugatskys are writing.

Another amusing touch is the mystery surrounding the head of the Institute, Janus Nevstruev. Nevstruev is actually two individuals—Janus-A, a young, efficient, unimaginative administrator, and Janus-U, an older scientist of considerable genius. Throughout the novel, the former bustles about keeping things in order while the latter turns up periodically amid his research into parallel universes. The most striking idiosyncrasy of Janus-U is his secure knowledge of the near future and a total ignorance of the recent past. The mystery remains unexplored and unanswered until the final chapters, when a group of researchers/magi figures out that the man is simultaneously traveling backward and forward in time. Significantly, Janus's last remarks to Privalov include a reference to some of the more outrageous speculations of quantum physics—a branch of science that easily rivals ancient mysticism in the unsettling picture of reality it provides.

Unfortunately, deft and witty touches such as these may not be enough to sustain the interest of most Western readers. The book is purposely loose and episodic, and the authors strive by and large for quick and temporary effects. As one can expect from a fantasy/satire, the characters are two-dimensional, essentially identified by single traits: the polite Eddie Amperian, the rude Victor Korneev, the dashing Cristobal Junta, the naive Privalov, etc. Though all readers of the brothers Strugatsky will find something entertaining somewhere in the novel, it simply lacks the depth and vision of the best earlier works, such as *Far Rainbow* and *Hard To Be a God*. It is thus a bit disappointing. In addition, much of the cultural tradition—the folklore, the satirical stereotypes, and so on—does not translate well. It deserves mention at this point that Soviet readers of the late sixties gave the book high marks; it was second only to *Hard To Be a God* as the most popular work of fantasy/science fiction in the Soviet Union.

In 1968 the Strugatskys published a sequel of sorts in *Skazka o troike—Tale of the Troika*. This much shorter novel begins with Privalov and the polite Amperian climbing aboard an unruly elevator to visit the rarely visited 76th floor of the Institute. Here there exists an entire fantasy world inhabited by Unexplained Phenomena. A state of emergency has arisen because this domain has apparently fallen into the hands of three men who were sent up to inspect the plumbing. They have been joined by the charlatan Vibegallo (here transliterated Vybegallo in the 1977 Macmillan and 1978 Pocket Books editions) in the role of scientific consultant.

The work is primarily a satire on the abuses of science and bureaucracy. The Troika clearly typifies the Bad Administrators, those self-serving wielders of power for its own sake that have been the target of scorn elsewhere in the Strugatsky canon. In the Troika we see bureaucratic malfeasance—and, incidentally, human short-sightedness—at its worst. The self-imposed function of this body is to "rationalize" all unexplained phenomena, paving the way for the "utilization" thereof. In fact, by "rationalizing," the Troika merely explains away the unexplainable, demonstrating in every case a complete lack of reason and comprehension and a preference for following forms and norms, no matter how narrow or absurd.

In their first confrontation with the Troika—in reality four men: Vuniuko, Khlebovvodov, Farfurkis, and Vybegallo—Privalov and Amperian witness the rationalization of a bogus invention, a typewriter that automatically answers questions. It only does so, however, when the grizzled old inventor is sitting at the keyboard. The dialogue that permeates this scene shares much with the zany absurdism of Kafka, the Marx brothers, and *Catch-22*. Privalov, who has a requisition for the Black Box (of information theory), ends up having the typewriter case forced upon him. He watches in agony as his doom is sealed by the Great Round Seal; he has no recourse once his requisition is stamped. In the world of this bureaucracy, nothing survives the Great Round Seal.

When they are not making bad decisions—or, more commonly, while they are in the process of doing so—the members of the Troika jockey for position. Particularly busy on this score are the wizened, punctilious Khlebovvodov and the swinish Farfurkis, who are forever fighting with one another for the favor of the dictatorial Vuniukov. Among the victims of their bureaucratic battling is Konstantin, a four-eyed, four-armed alien from Antares who is seeking assistance in the repair of his space ship. Both Khlebovvodov and Farfurkis try to impress Vuniukov by stubbornly refusing to accept Konstantin as an alien, despite his appearance, his technology, and his ability to read minds and fly around the room on his own power. Ultimately, none of these rigid, conservative, myopic men will risk embracing anything that does not suit their own narrow concept of reality, a reality bounded by the blank walls of their chamber, their rule books, and their petty ambitions.

A number of touches suggest that the Strugatskys are at least in part aiming their barbs at Soviet bureaucracy in particular. In the course of attempting to one-up each other, the members of the Troika frequently fall back on patriotic nonsense. For instance, in excoriating the Troika's perpetual scapegoat, Commandant Zubo, at one point, Farfurkis complains that the educational system in the Colony of Unexplained Phenomena is not doing its job: "There are almost no political education lectures. The visual aids in agitation reflect yesterday's lessons....The slogan-making industry has fallen into neglect," etc. [Pocket Books, 1978; p. 218]. There are frequent burlesques of the bureaucrats' usage of catch-words like "the people" and "the struggle," for example: "Today's youth does not struggle enough, does not pay enough attention to the struggle, has no desire to struggle more, to struggle to make struggling the true, primary goal of the struggle..." [p. 236].

This is not to say that this novelette is to be taken as a wholesale criticism of the communist system. What the Strugatskys lament here, as elsewhere, is the failure of human beings to exercise the best aspects of their humanity, giving in instead to selfishness, pettiness, stupidity, and a too restrictive orthodoxy. This point is underlined in a few relatively more straightforward passages scattered throughout the work. In more than one spot, Eddie Amperian takes advantage of the "humanizer," an apparatus that draws forth the more humane and rational aspects of the targeted individual. Under the influence of the "humanizer," Vuniukov confesses the weakness and vanity of the

Troika, faults that reflect a humankind too recently emerged "from a state of constant warfare, from a world of bloodshed and violence, from a world of lies, baseness, and greed," and thus unable to rise above suspicion, egotism, and narrow-mindedness [p. 214].

In such rare rational moments, it is evident that the Strugatskys are again criticizing human weakness rather than any innate malevolence. Environment once more proves to be the strongest influence on man's nature. Indeed, by the story's end even Privalov and Amperian find themselves seduced by the petty insanity of this world; Privalov is talking himself into competing with Farfurkis and Khlebovvodov for Vuniukov's favor and a good salary, while Amperian is figuring out how to replace Vybegallo. Only a *deus ex machina* in the form of two colleagues from below saves them. The Troika is precipitously dissolved amid thunder and smoke, although the incorrigible Vuniukov, as he departs, announces in typical parliamentary fashion, "There is an opinion that we shall meet again in another place and at another time" [p. 257].

The conclusion is just open-ended enough to reflect the moral of other Strugatsky works: that it is extremely difficult, if not impossible, to erase permanently the human propensity for selfishness and vice. What was true in *Hard To Be a God* is true in the much different setting of *Troika*; no matter how strong one's convictions and values, they can only function properly in a like milieu. The individual is largely at the mercy of his social surroundings.

In keeping with the madcap pace of the whole work, this conclusion comes upon the reader without warning. Nothing that leads up to it suggests that Privalov and Amperian will capitulate to the Troika; by contrast, consider Anton-Rumata's gradual fall from social/spiritual superiority. Such inconsistencies in character, like those of plot and even tone, would be glaring faults in something more serious. Since *Troika*, like *Monday*, does not pretend to take itself seriously, one must approach it on its own terms. On the level of a satirical cartoon, *Troika* works; it has moments of genuine humor and incisive wit. But much of it is, like all of *Monday*, merely clever or playful. Both books are well within the boundaries of Soviet popular culture, a realm that reaches from rural folklore to the urban-oriented magazine of satire, *Krokodil*. Only when comparing these two novels with the likes of *Noon, Far Rainbow*, and *Hard To Be a God* must one conclude that they are a long way from the most effective fiction of these authors. They must be read just for fun.

A much subtler form of satire appears in another 1968 novelette, *Vtoroe nashestvie marsian*. This has appeared in English as *The Second Martian Invasion* (London: MacGibbon & Kee, 1970), as *Second War of the Worlds* (Macmillan, 1973), and most recently as *The Second Invasion from Mars* (Macmillan, 1979; Collier, 1980). As one of these titles shows, this work looks back in a skewed way at Wells's *War of the Worlds*. The differences between this story and Wells's, however, are greater than the titular similarity, which, as will be seen, is ironic.

This Martian invasion takes place in a contemporary storybook-land that commingles the ancient and the modern. Its village of fools is an updated version of the settings of much nineteenth-century Russian literature, except that the characters possess names out of Greek mythology (Phoebus Apollo, Polyphemus, Artemis, etc.) while, on the other hand, retaining memories of World War II, Blackshirts, and Albert Einstein. This is not modern Greece, however; these people are distinctly northern European in their habits. This mixture of eras and cultures suggests that the characters are intended to be universal representatives of humanity. Indeed, the story is pure fable.

It is related through the diary of Phoebus Apollo; despite his name, he is merely a retired teacher and amateur scientist with a passion for collecting stamps, padding his pension, and recording the trivia of everyday life. He has tendencies toward hypochondria, pomposity, cowardice, and rationalization: his propensity for self-exaltation and self-justification makes him occasionally unreliable as a narrator, though his rhetoric generally fails to disguise the truth.

What Apollo narrates is a sequence of episodes that transpire over a couple of weeks in June of an unspecified year. In distinct contrast to the satirical fantasies handled so far, this narrative is no headlong rush from one delirious situation to another, but a gradual, naturalistic unfolding of events. It begins dramatically with an eruption of red light in the sky one night, an occurrence quickly overrun by the subsequent rumors—everything from fireworks to a factory explosion to nuclear war—and by the petty details of town life. One of the ironies of the story, in fact, is that as the drama proceeds such details continue to dominate Apollo's narrative. We learn early of the infidelities of Apollo's married daughter, ironically named Artemis after the virgin goddess of the hunt, of her political activist husband Charon, of the perpetually drunk cesspool cleaner Minotaur who is forever running his truck into public buildings, and of the policeman Polyphemus, forever self-important and forever taunted by the crowd of men that inhabits the village tavern. We learn only gradually of the "invasion" that has followed the red skies of the first paragraphs.

By the fourth day following the initial incident, the rumors have given way to the widespread belief that the Martians have landed. Knowing as an amateur scientist that Mars supports no intelligent life, Apollo expresses contempt for this latest rumor, though he does check at the post office to see if the alleged invaders have issued any stamps to add to his collection. Shortly hereafter arises the first peculiar hint of what is to come: it is revealed that a locally based colonel has lectured his soldiers on the patriotic duty of caring for their gastric juices. That day all the newspapers feature articles contradicting the scientific evidence against life on Mars and others promoting the importance of healthy stomach juices.

Obsessed with his own purely personal concerns, such as his pension, Apollo notes only in passing subsequent unsettling events: the supplanting of the local wheat crop with an alien blue variety, the sudden appearance of mysterious young men in tight-fitting coats, and the establishment of mobile stations where villagers can donate their stomach juice in exchange for currency. Soon thereafter, Apollo witnesses the kidnapping of the corrupt, unpopular mayor by a group of the young men. Once it is evident that these "Martians" are in control, Apollo's first act is to approach one concerning his pension; before he can speak, he is somehow struck unconscious.

Even after stomach juice is declared the official currency, Apollo has little trouble accepting the odd state of affairs. Hearing that the mayor has been "exterminated" and his estate turned into a permanent station for the collection of stomach juice, he asserts, "I approve and support it. I always stand for permanence and stability" [Collier edition, p. 196]. Thus, when he stumbles upon an insurgent assault on a Martian automobile, he takes the side of the local farmers who counterattack and hand the guerrillas over to the Martians; the farmers, of course, are profiting nicely from the new blue wheat. By this point, even the tavern super-patriot, the one-legged veteran Polyphemus, has tempered his anti-Martian fervor and is donating stomach juice; all that remains of his earlier rhetoric is a concern that the aliens are not giving them fair remuneration. Blue beer and blue bread are becoming staples of the town's diet. And when Apollo finally donates stomach juice himself, he finds the money a handsome addition to his pension.

The story's climax comes as a calm dialectical exchange between Apollo and his insurgent, intellectual son-in-law Charon, who has reappeared after a long absence following his arrest by farmers and a generous release by the Martians. Charon laments mankind's easy capitulation to Martian overlordship and catalogues all that will be lost—schools, laboratories, progress in general. Man is now no more than "a factory of stomach juice" who has traded his intelligence, independence, and star-probing curiosity for "a handful of coppers." "Not in the boom of a cosmic catastrophe," he says in Apollo's paraphrase, "not in the flames of nuclear war and not even in the clutches of overpopulation would the history of mankind come to an end, but, don't you see, in calm, sated tranquility" [p. 226].

Ironically, after summarizing this peroration, Apollo remarks that he "understand[s] abstract reasoning poorly" and only found Charon's comments depressing. He goes on the offensive with the narrowly pragmatic justification that the average person needs "coppers" more than he needs social ideals. He argues, furthermore, that humanity has not been reduced to slavery but has achieved a previously unrealized worth in the sudden value of its gastric juices. Charon, laughing with some bitterness, observes that the Martians had told him the same thing. His point is wholly lost on Apollo.

Apollo obviously represents Everyman in this situation—thickheaded, short-sighted, willing to sell himself if the price is right and then rationalize the act. Unfortunately, in his assertions regarding humankind's preference for comfort over ideals, he is absolutely correct. Charon, on the other hand, is the lone, intelligent revolutionary, reminiscent of the hapless rebel leader Arata in *Hard To Be a God*. His position is clearly the more sympathetic one; that it comes across as such despite Apollo's wrong-headed viewpoint is a clever rhetorical stroke on the authors' part.

Indeed, esthetically and thematically, the best element in the story is the contrast between Apollo's tone and the reader's perception of the events, which overlays with comedy an otherwise nightmarish tale of subjugation. In the work's conclusion, with the Martian takeover complete and the military in the process of demobilization, the social fabric of Apollo's world remains largely unaltered: he continues to pursue his daily concerns and drink with the men at the tavern, except now they drink blue beer in the company of Martians in tight-fitting coats. Everything has changed; nothing has changed.

The message of this fable contains little new to the reader familiar with the authors' other work. It restates what has been said elsewhere: that the human animal has an unfortunate tendency to accept short-term satisfactions—profit, power, comfort—at the expense of his long-range potential for individual and social progress. What *is* different in this work is the means used to convey the message: a smooth, traditional Russian blend of fantasy and reality. Though here, as in the tales of the Privalov universe, the characters are burlesques, they are at least more credible, in the sense that, say, Dickens's characters are credible. *The Second Invasion from Mars* must be considered a modest success—modest, that is, in its relative unpretentiousness and familiarity.

The Strugatskys' one other novel of 1968, *Ulitka na sklone—The Snail on the Slope*—is in many respects the consummate fable of this phase; it combines the mad atmosphere and fantastic images of the Privalov stories with the careful construction of *Invasion*. Unlike the others, however, *The Snail on the Slope* does not yield its underlying message so readily.

The novel actually consists of two tales that proceed on parallel courses in alternating chapters. In the first chapter we meet Pepper, a young artist-intellectual caught within the confines of a bureaucracy called the Directorate. The Directorate compound sits on a cliff overlooking a massive, mist-shrouded Forest; in fact, its stated *raison d'etre* is to study the Forest and eventually eradicate it by taming the area into a park suitable for civilization, a task which suggests the rationalization-*cum*-civilization syndrome of *Tale of the Troika*. On the other hand, Pepper, with his artistic sensibilities, loves the Forest from afar, idealizes it, and longs to penetrate its mysteries. Unfortunately, he can get neither the permission to enter the Forest nor a means of returning home to "the Mainland." He is trapped.

Kandid, introduced in the second chapter, lives in the heart of the Forest. Formerly an employee of the Directorate, he lost his memory and his way when his helicopter crashed during a reconnaissance expedition. He too is trapped—in the primitive, provincial conditions of a Forest village. Though he has managed to recollect bits of his former life, they are just enough to make him yearn for the world high on the cliff which he left behind. The natives—a backward, superstitious, and particularly long-winded lot—treat him as the village idiot; they call him "Dummy," and have mated him with a local girl, Nava, of similarly unknown origin. Kandid wants nothing more than to find his way out of the Forest to the so-called "Devil Rocks," the Directorate, but can find no one disciplined or adventurous enough to assist him through the Forest's maze of paths and dangers.

Pepper's struggles with the civilized bureaucracy and Kandid's with the primeval Forest proceed with near perfect counterpoint. The two quests mirror and complement each other in what must be regarded as one of the brothers' most dialectical, if least conclusive, fables.

The reigning spirit in Pepper's story seems to be Kafka. Pepper finds himself constantly victimized by the arbitrary and even whimsical power of the Directorate. In Chapter Three, for instance, after we have seen him frustrated in his attempts to either reach the Forest or return home, he is suddenly evicted from his room by a frightened hotel manager when his visa expires. He recalls having earlier been singled out for harassment, when "[n]inety-two denunciations of me, all written in one hand and with different signatures" had arrived at the desk of a friend in the bureaucracy.

Later in the same chapter, Pepper is passing time in an office building when the announcement comes that the director will address all personnel over the telephone. Immediately all work halts as everyone around Pepper picks up a receiver and listens intently. Pepper, afraid that he alone is "missing something again," grabs at any free phone he can find. When he finally comes across one that is operating, he can make no sense of the message. A petty bureaucrat of his acquaintance, one Hausbotcher, informs him coldly that that phone is not meant for him. Pepper flies wildly through the adjoining offices, seeking his own personal phone and failing.

Pepper's friend Kim eventually arranges for him to meet the director in order to sort out his problems with the bureaucracy, but when Pepper shows up at the appropriate office (in Chapter Five), he is treated to an even more Kafkaesque series of frustrations. Shunted from waiting room to waiting room, handed to an official who Pepper thinks is the director until he reveals he is the personnel manager, Pepper is finally ordered to report to a vehicle outside that is actually heading into the Forest. He barely finds his way out in time through a bewildering chain of halls and rooms.

In Kafka, such multilayered and impenetrable bureaucracies commonly stand between the protagonists and the ultimate understanding or accceptance they seek. The same is happening here; for Pepper, the Forest embodies the meaning of life. For the Directorate, as Pepper hears during the director's scrambled phone address, "The meaning of life does not exist, nor does the meaning of action" [p. 81, unpublished Bantam edition]. The Directorate is not interested in truly understanding the Forest, "life," or anything. Instead, it is "fond of so-called simple solutions, libraries, internal communications, geographical and other maps" [p. 82]. Like any other bureaucracy, in other words, its primary function is self-perpetuation. Whatever ostensibly scientific purpose it may originally have had has been lost. Of course, it also has no moral or ethical impetus either. As we have seen elsewhere in the Strugatskys' work, research and progress must have solid moral foundations or they produce more harm than good. The Directorate is a construct of misguided human reason. "Reason does not blush or suffer pangs of conscience," Pepper hears over the phone, "[i]t is deceitful and slippery, it is impermanent and dissimulates" [p. 82].

Ironically, when Pepper finally does reach the Forest, the experience fails to fulfill his hopes. Indeed, alongside his initial inarticulate wonder, he finds the Forest "nauseating." This reaction hardly surprises the reader who has been following Kandid's attempts to escape the overwhelming and even oppressive life of the Forest. "Life" here means, ambiguously, not just growth and reproduction but the concomitant death and decay, which are, after all, life processes themselves. The Forest is not the understanding, benign parent Pepper seeks; at best it is indifferent if not, in places, malevolent. Dominated by their surroundings, the residents of Kandid's village are almost literally people of the earth—living in ant-infested mud huts, feeding off fungus, fermented vegetation and even edible turf, given to ignorance, narrow-mindedness, superstition, and fear.

Their environment provides plenty of justification for such tendencies. Among the threatening phenomena with which these people have to contend are "deadlings." These are vaguely humanoid but non-human life forms with brightly-hued, burning hot hides, round heads, hollow eyes, and long arms with which they grab women and haul them away into the forest depths—to eat them, the villagers presume. During the course of the introductory "Kandid" section (Chapter Two), there are also ominous references to villages full of strange folk and lakes covered with drowned bodies, to Maidens and the Accession and a whole landscape of peculiar terrors beyond the edge of the village. None of these prevents Kandid from finally taking off on his own, followed by his wife Nava.

We do not begin to learn how real, and how bizarre, are the phenomena of this fetid realm until Pepper's visit in the pivotal Chapter

66

Six. At the biostation to which Pepper has been transported to receive his pay, the worlds of Forest and Directorate intersect. Pepper's first close encounter with "life" in the Forest takes place during the so-called eruption of a natural cesspit. This foul-smelling pool, a seething mess of protoplasm that digests everything that falls into it, including a motorcycle, reproduces by spitting out a few dozen blobs of "whitish rippling goo," which parade off into the vegetation. This is not the confrontation with the meaning of life that the idealist Pepper expected. He quickly concludes that he is incapable of understanding the Forest: "I've been here, understood nothing, found nothing I wanted to find, but I know now that I never will understand anything....There's nothing in common between the Forest and me, the Forest is no nearer to me than the Directorate" [p. 140].

Pepper is alone in his existential alienation, as he was alone in his search for ultimate meaning. For his comrades, Directorate employees all, the Forest biostation is just another place where they can swap women, get drunk, and indulge in other less specified vices. Even the most ambitious researchers are concerned with printing articles, not understanding the Forest. During his brief sojourn at the biostation, Pepper's dislike of the Directorate turns to disgust, and his disgust with the Forest to fear. By the end of the chapter, Pepper—disillusioned and *angstvoll*—wants nothing but to be far from both Forest and Directorate.

The two chapters that follow mark the analogous climax of Kandid's quest, a climax that is more revealing if no more fulfilling for the protagonist. Here the narrative becomes absolutely surreal, as Kandid and Nava stumble upon a village that seems deserted, though in fact it is full of men in a state of suspended animation. When night comes on, a bright lilac fog fills the village, people come to life, and Kandid finds himself in the midst of an inexplicable, dream-like ritual during which he nearly loses Nava. In the morning, Nava awakes with a scalpel in her hand—in her dim-witted ignorance, she thinks it a creature that crawled there—and the two of them witness the drowning of the village.

Traveling on, they encounter other strange scenes: a warm lake where dozens of naked women float, a fog-covered hill that gives birth to wave after wave of insects and monsters. The grotesque flavor of this world is suggested in a description of the latter episode.

Only the slugs remained on the hilltop. In their place came spilling down the slopes the most incredible animals—hairies came rolling, clumsy arm-chewers came lurching down on frail legs, and there were plenty of others unknown as yet, speckled, multi-eyed, naked, shining half-beast, half-insects. Then the silence again, then the process started up once more, and again, and again, in a frightening, urgent rhythm, an inexorable energy....[D]eadlings came running out from time to time and at once rushed into the Forest, leaving white trails of steam in their wake. And the motionless lilac cloud kept swallowing and spitting out, swallowing and spitting out, tireless and regular as a machine [Bantam, p. 168].

All of the above, we learn—the drowned village, the lake, the hill—belong to the Accession. Soon Kandid and Nava meet up with the overseers of the Accession—the Maidens. These strapping, domineering women have absolute command over the life forces of the Forest. One of them, it turns out, is Nava's long-lost mother. It quickly becomes clear that the Maidens have no use for men; they reproduce in their own mysterious way via the warm lakes viewed earlier. The goal of their Accession is nothing less than the gradual eradication of male-dominated civilization, be it Forest village or, it is hinted, Directorate outpost. The task of the deadlings, their servants, is to gather up all the women in the Forest to join them. Kandid's discovery of the truth behind the Accession is his turning point; he loses Nava but learns he can kill a deadling with a vertical slash of the new-found scalpel.

The last three chapters are anti-climactic for both men, though much happens in them. Pepper returns to the Directorate and awakes amid chaos: a machine with a built-in self-destruct device has gotten loose. For most of the episode, Pepper hides out and overhears a dream discussion between several machines on the subjects of work and humanity. The next morning he discovers he has been made the director. Unwillingly yanked to the apex of his world, Pepper still finds himself at the mercy of its arbitrary absurdities; he refuses to sign a directive making chance occurrences crimes only to have taken seriously his sardonic suggestion that the eradication engineers eradicate themselves by committing suicide.

On a less humorous front, Kandid has returned to his village to warn the inhabitants about the nature of the Accession, only to be laughed off. To them he is still just the village idiot, though they are impressed by his new talent for destroying deadlings. Curiously, he persists in his personal war against the Accession even as he admits to himself that it represents the inevitable wave of the future, a historical necessity like revolution. What he resents most is being left out.

Pepper and Kandid are both examples of a familiar Strugatsky type—the committed intellectual who is trapped and ultimately compromised by his environment. Darko Suvin, in his introductory essay to the unpublished Bantam edition of the novel, suggests that they represent "the two horns of the alternative facing modern intellectuals...: *accommodation* and *refusal*" [p. 19]. Suvin is correct only if one views the Accession as representing the same abuses of power as the Directorate. It is true that, despite the great contrasts between the two worlds, they are in many ways mirror images of one another, reversed but analogous. Even though one realm is dominated by men, regulation, and runaway technology and the other by women, tradition, and runaway "life," in both progress equals destruction; in both, the lack of moral and intellectual courage leads to social stagnation. But one must bear in mind that at bottom there are not just two opposing entities, Forest and Directorate, but three: the Directorate, the Accession, and the Native Population or villagers. Seen in this light, the village and the bureaucracy represent opposing forms of social stagnation, and the only "progressive" action taking place on any front is the strangely regressive one of the Accession. If it has any ethical foundation, it is not accessible to human reason, a theme that looks ahead to *The Ugly Swans*. Both Pepper and Kandid end up accepting, even if reluctantly and superficially, the world-views of their respective social contexts—i.e., bureaucracy and village—and both to some extent in reaction against the revolting alienness of the Forest.

Diana Greene, in a 1986 article, takes a feminist critical approach to this novel and finds, not surprisingly, a disgust for all things female. She points out that the Maidens of the Forest are manipulative and merciless, that their Accession, as described, is horrible, and that the female characters, from Kandid's Nava to the various servants of the Directorate in Pepper's tale, are dim-witted, shrewish, or untrustworthy. This criticism could be taken as serious evidence of sexism on the Strugatskys' part if the male characters were any more attractive. In fact, however, all the village characters of the Forest are stupid and ob-

69

noxious, as—in their different way—are all those of the Directorate, regardless of gender. If anything, the Maidens of the Accession are at least disciplined and effective in their pursuit, which cannot be said of the male-dominated societies of village and Directorate.

It should be evident that this work abounds in ambiguities and subtleties, far too many to treat thoroughly here. If *The Second Invasion from Mars* is more satisfying in its seductive simplicity, *The Snail on the Slope* is richer and more thought-provoking. Like the other fables in the satirical fantasy vein, it seems to be primarily concerned with the fallible response of the human mind and its institutions to the challenges of its environment and particularly to the unknown, the domain that science purports to explore. In all of these, we have seen the best impulses of the human spirit crippled by self-aggrandizement, ignorance, conservatism, and bureaucratic inefficiency; we have seen the apparently inexplicable explained away ("rationalized") and misused ("utilized"). This fiction has been laced with motifs from Russian folklore and literature and with touches of Swift, Kafka, and Carroll. Also, the handling of man's difficulty in comprehending the alien, particularly in *Invasion* and *Snail*, points to the influence of Stanislaw Lem. It is this theme that dominates their latest work.

V.

CONFRONTING THE ALIEN

Over the course of the sixties, the dialectical fables of the brothers Strugatsky grew more fabulous, while their dialectic grew less positivistic, more punctured by ambiguity and doubt. It is a long way from the future certainties of *Noon* to the dubious reality of *The Snail on the Slope*, a long way from the philanthropic optimism of the Gorbovsky universe to the dark satire of Pepper's world. This esthetic/philosophical evolution in the Strugatskys' fiction reached its culmination in a group of works that appeared in the early seventies.

The first of these, *Gadkie lebedi*—in English, *The Ugly Swans*—was originally scheduled for Soviet publication in 1968, but was pulled at the last minute. It did not come into print until 1972, in an unauthorized edition from Frankfurt, West Germany. Though apparently composed in the same period as *The Second Invasion from Mars* and *The Snail on the Slope*, it does not partake so heavily of the fantastic and the satirical; instead, it points ahead to the more serious concerns and approaches of later work.

Swans takes place in a time much like the present, in a rural community of some carefully unspecified European country. The protagonist, a hard-bitten, hard-drinking writer in the Hemingway tradition named Victor Banev, has returned to his hometown to take over the care of his daughter Irma from his ex-wife. He finds the town rotting from three years of unbroken rain. This phenomena is attributed to the inmates of a nearby leper colony, known contemptuously as "slimies" or "four-eyes" since their form of the disease imparts a slimy yellow cast to the skin, particularly in large rings around the eyes. Individual slimies can be found occasionally around the town, usually at night; they dress completely in black—overcoats, hats, gloves, even to black bandages that cover all of the face but the ringed eyes. It is also evident that they exercise considerable control over the children and teenagers of the town. The townspeople, typically, react with fear and hatred to this manifestation of the abnormal in their midst; early in the book, we see slimies beaten and kidnapped by local fascist thugs and caught in man traps set by a town official. Yet despite frequent comparisons of the slimies to other victims of persecution—Blacks, Jews, intellectuals—they never come across as particularly sympathetic beings. Besides their ghastly physical appearance, they are cold, insensitive, and arrogant, even to those who risk a great deal to protect them.

Such ambiguities fill this problematic tale, beginning with the aforementioned lack of specificity of setting. The society depicted contains elements of both East and West. Like Banev, most of the characters have names that are Slavic or otherwise Eastern European. The government is ostensibly democratic, with a president and a parliament, both much maligned by the dissident hero, and the economic system is reportedly based on social Darwinism, suggesting Western capitalism. On the other hand, the number of domestic spies and counterspies operating throughout the story and the hint of distant labor camps are all reminiscent of Stalinism, though they could reflect fascism as well. In at least one place, where he speaks of wars of liberation and imperialism, the president sounds like a communist leader, though elsewhere it is made quite clear that the country is anti-communist; the non-leper who oversees the leper colony, one Golem, is a social outcast because he is an avowed Marxist. At bottom, it is a society with few virtues and many vices, overrun by public corruption and private cynicism. Ultimately, it could be any system; even Soviet society, as the Strugatskys are obviously aware, has persecuted its share of Jews and intellectuals. One could point to this ambiguity as one reason the book never saw Soviet publication.

Another ambiguous and possibly controversial touch is the characters, particularly the hero. If the cautious, relaxed Leonid Gorbovsky and his comrades were not heroic enough for the "cold stream" critics, they were angels compared to the boozing, womanizing, sardonic Victor Banev. From the novel's beginning, we know him as an intellectual dissident who has long carried on a personal campaign against Mr. President. He is unpatriotic and anti-military (though decorated for heroism in World War II); he is perpetually drunk and involved in a purely physical affair with a socially active nurse, Diana. His speech is often profane, cruelly ironic, and even misanthropic. Yet at the foundation of Banev's pugnacious personality lies a real passion for justice and a genuine despair at humankind's inability to raise itself above animal selfishness and shortsightedness. Victor's apparent misanthropism—so counter to the humane optimism one finds in early creations like Gorbovsky and Zhilin—thus has its roots in a similar concern for humanity's well-being; Victor Banev, however, lacks the Marxist confidence of the others. For this reason, he is a more complex and interesting figure than his predecessors.

Worse are Victor's frequent drinking partners, the hopelessly alcoholic Quadriga, an artist who has sold out to the system, and the sanitation inspector Pavor. Most of their conversation, usually in the company of the above-mentioned Golem, is ironic, cynical, and harsh, but amid the wisecracks and obscenities a number of surprisingly serious observations get made. At one point, for instance, Pavor expounds at length upon the biological and ideological bankruptcy of the human species, "this rotting pile of shit." Much of what he says, misanthropic though it is, rings true until his jeremiad degenerates into crypto-fascism, ending with his recommendation that the masses be destroyed. Shortly thereafter, Golem reveals to Victor that Pavor is in fact a government agent out after the slimies and anyone associated with them. Later in the novel, Victor takes overt, if morally ambiguous, action by betraying Pavor to military intelligence, which is protecting the slimies for its own sinister purposes, then standing by as he is arrested and hauled away, not to be seen again. Even taking a moral stance in this corrupt world does not free one from the law of the jungle.

The harsh flavor of setting, character, and dialogue in this book is exemplified by the following scene; here Victor is hustling his daughter Irma to the apartment of his lover Diana, through a gauntlet of whores, low-lifes, and lechers, the worst of the latter a drunken parliamentarian named Rosheper. When Rosheper directs a sexual remark to Irma, Banev knocks him down and hurries the girl on to Diana's door.

> He started knocking wildly, and Diana responded at once. "Go to hell," she shrieked. "You stinking impotent, you dirty asshole, you piece of dogshit!"
>
> "Diana!" barked Victor. "Open up!"
>
> Diana fell silent, and the door opened. She stood at the threshold, French umbrella positioned for the attack. Victor shoved her back, dragged Irma into the room, and slammed the door.

"So it's you," said Diana. "I thought it was Rosheper again." She smelled of liquor. "Oh, God," she said. "Who is this?"

"This is my daughter," said Victor with effort....

He looked fixedly at Diana with desperation and hope. It seemed, thank God, that she wasn't completely drunk....

"You must be out of your mind," she said softly.

"She's wet," he said. "Get her into something dry, put her to bed, and—"

"I won't," Irma announced.

"Irma," said Victor. "Kindly listen or I'll wallop you."

"Somebody here deserves to get walloped," said Diana hopelessly [Collier, 1979; p. 97].

The ambiguities of setting, character, and moral tone are consonant with the ambiguity of the novel's theme. This, in turn, is bound up in the fundamental nature and identity of the slimies. It is clear early in the narrative, through their control of the climate and the children, who have become prodigies under the tutelage of the slimies, that these beings, though human-born, are somewhat more than human. Their "yellow leprosy" is less a disease than a feature of their election to the ranks of supermen. Other marks of this status are the previously mentioned emotional frigidity and arrogance. Their insensitivity to the human life around them, with the notable exception of the young, extends even to the local thugs who persecute them; they are wholly uninterested in punishing the offenders. They are coldly, even cruelly, rational and are apparently training the children to be the same.

Victor discovers this fact in a most personal way when the children, through his daughter Irma, ask him to speak at their school. The questions and responses he receives from his young audience are not at all what he expects; though they claim to respect him, they are unsparing in their criticism of his hard-bitten heroes and the modern ethic he depicts in his fiction. They question his ideas of progress and justice, in terms he considers insolent. Yet he cannot help feeling, and fearing, that these children are correct in their way. They do not care about the mistakes of the past or about building upon them for the future. They want to turn their backs entirely on the old order and begin completely anew. Frozen before his listeners at one point, Victor asks himself, "Has the new age really dawned?...It seemed that the future had really managed to extend its feelers into the very heart of the present, and that that future was cold and pitiless" [Collier, 1980; p. 74-75].

This is the problem that haunts the protagonist up through the climactic final confrontation of the old world and the new in the ninth chapter (of twelve). Following the sudden disappearance of the entire population of youngsters, the townspeople, led by the local police and the handful of gold-shirted fascist thugs, mob the entrance of the leprosarium. At first they are unable to enter the colony because of the barbed wire and armed soldiers surrounding it. Just when it looks as though the guards might be overwhelmed by the crowd, a god-like voice speaks up over the incessant rain, a voice "like thunder...from all sides at once....It was the voice of someone huge, arrogant, and scornful, standing with his back to the crowd and addressing it over his shoulder; the voice of someone engaged in important work and irritated, finally, by some trifle" [p. 160-161]. It explains, calmly but forcefully, that the children left of their own free will, "because you had become totally disagreeable to them. They no longer wish to live the way you live and the way your forebears lived" [p. 161]. The lecture continues a little longer, then the Voice orders everyone home with a convincing shove from a cold, wet gust of wind. And, demoralized, the people leave.

Victor reacts to this episode with mixed feelings. On the one hand, he appreciates the humiliation of the fascists and the mob; on the other, he was part of that crowd of distressed parents himself—he lost Irma to the slimies—and he finds the whole incident insulting in retrospect. The slimies, as supermen, are more merciless than the children in Victor's audience. Victor reminds himself that despite the mess humanity has made of the world, there is a warmth in human relationships that no system premised on strict reason can replace. The slimies apparently have no human feelings, including sexual ones, and Victor cannot bear the thought of such a world, even if he can acknowledge its merits. He tries to decide on the spot whether he is for or against the slimies. On the against side he lists their contemptuous elitism, their "cruelty, arrogance, inhumanity, physical deformity." In their favor, they have the support of those he loves and respects the most—Golem, Diana, Irma, and the other intelligent young people. The slimies are also superintellectuals themselves and seem to have the best interests of the children in mind.

The slimies are, of course, the "ugly swans," the more developed form of the species, but one—reversing the Hans Christian Andersen tale—that is less attractive than the duckling from which it emerged. Indeed, late in the novel Golem refers to Victor more than once as a "beautiful duckling," that is, a more humanly appealing but less evolved being. As supermen, the slimies so transcend the human stock from which they grew that they have become, in effect, aliens, with alien minds, viewpoints, and powers. As such, their true natures and objectives must remain difficult if not impossible for mere humans to understand. These beings are the catalysts bringing on the future, but only by wholly rejecting the old humanity, with all its vices and virtues. As Golem remarks, "Nature doesn't deceive, it fulfills its promises, only not the way we thought and often not the way we would have liked" [p. 193].

As the populace flees the town following the climax, Victor stays behind to watch the New Order unfold. It is not, as he had once feared, like the Nazi New Order, a ruthless displacement of one group by another. Instead, the rain disappears, the sun emerges, and the town simply evaporates. There is no trace of the slimies either, but Irma and her boyfriend Bol-Kunats, both suddenly and prematurely adults, walk hand in hand through the new spring. Irma playfully aims a twig at a fighter jet passing far overhead as it disappears into the sun. Victor has to acknowledge the benevolence of the new world, though he reminds himself, in the book's last line, that he does not belong there. To recall an allusion made earlier in the novel, he is like the crippled boy left behind when the Pied Piper led the children to paradise.

The Ugly Swans provides an unusual solution to the problem of the disjuncture between humankind's utopian hopes and its seemingly irremediable weaknesses. Even in a work like *Hard To Be a God*, man's future still seems viable, though only after innumerable struggles to better himself. In *Swans*, however, as to some extent in *The Snail on the Slope*, mankind as we know it is simply eliminated from the picture. It could be argued that these are metaphors for the ultimate revolution prophesied by Marxist theory, except that in each case the new order represents not the triumph of the masses but their total disfranchisement by a more-than-human elite. In *Swans*, at least, this sweep meets with the qualified approval of the protagonist and, it appears, the authors. Victor Banev represents the endpoint of a trend that began as far back as *Hard To Be a God*: the committed intellectual who replaces Everyman as people's hero and champion of utopian thought. Unfortunately, as an intellectual, he is too aware of man's fallibility to take progress on faith. So, clearly, are the Strugatskys.

With its moral ambiguity and thematic complexity, with its vivid, realistic characters, the novel is as much a contribution to modern literature as it is a remarkable work of science fiction. The same can be said for the short novel *Piknik na obochine*, published originally in 1972 and later in English as *Roadside Picnic*. It also dramatizes humankind's encounter with the alien and the error-ridden methods utilized to come to terms with it.

Picnic takes place in a Canadian community named Harmont, the nearest the Strugatskys have come to a frankly American setting. Harmont is one of six places world-wide that have experienced a "visitation" by extraterrestrials who came and went without being seen, but who left behind artifacts of their visit in autocircumscribed Zones. The Zones are full of grotesque dangers for the unwary, and even for the cautious "stalkers," the self-reliant thieves who sneak illegally into the alien territory to spirit out items that sell well on the insatiable black market.

The main character, Red (from Redrick) Schuhart, is such a man. We first meet him as a young lab assistant, already with a criminal record as a stalker, working at the research institute that stands at the edge of the Harmont Zone. We see him at his most cocksure and insolent in this chapter, as he guides his superior, the scientist Kirill, and another greenhorn into the Zone to search for a specific item in what was once a motor pool garage. In this episode the reader first becomes acquainted with the sort of bizarre pitfalls awaiting humans in the Zone. At first, the main danger seems to be the sudden concentrations of gravity that can instantly flatten anyone or anything. Once they reach the garage, however, Kirill accidentally backs into a silver web, unfamiliar to Red, which promptly disappears. Kirill seems fine all the way back to the lab, but an hour later he is found dead of cardiac arrest.

In each of the story's four chapters, we learn more about the alien horrors of the Zone, although we remain as ignorant as the characters themselves of the original uses of the cosmic litter. Among the items Red sneaks out of the Zone during a haul in the second chapter, for instance, are an assortment of "needles" (tiny spikes that flash with photoenergy), "empties" (each consisting of two disks a firm half-meter apart, with nothing between them), and a small ring that once set spinning will continue indefinitely. These and other artifacts are filtered through a violence-ridden underworld to end up in the hands of scientists, private collectors, big business, the military, and anyone else with the money to pay for them. A few items, such as a tiny storage cell that reproduces and never runs out of energy, have found wide commercial applications. Some, like a burning blue substance called "witches' jelly" that consumes anything it touches, have frightening potential. Most of the artifacts remain pure mysteries. As one character puts it, even where man has found applications for the alien technology, he is probably "hammering nails with microscopes."

Then there are side effects of the Zones that seem to have nothing to do with the actual artifacts. One is the resurrection of corpses from the town cemetery. Another, even less explicable, is that whenever someone who was living near a Zone at the time of the Visitation takes up residence elsewhere, the new community experiences a string of unprecedented disasters. Yet another effect is mutations, not traceable to radiation, in the children fathered by stalkers. Red's daughter, for example, is born with a covering of thick brown fur, which earns her the affectionate name "Monkey." She seems otherwise normal as a child, but by the third chapter, when she has reached puberty, she has lost the art of human speech and reason; she is essentially an ape. By this time the other consequences of life at the Zone have come home to Red: he has spent several more years in prison for stalking, a new law prevents him or any Zone resident from relocating, and the corpse of Red's father has moved in to join his pathetic family.

One of the worst of the Visitation's deleterious effects, however, is not at all alien—quite the contrary. It is the all-too-human drive to exploit, abuse, and victimize for personal gain. A prominent feature of the story is the hierarchy of thieves, gangsters, and other middlemen that surround the main characters, all of them with ties to the respectable world of officialdom, science, and the military-industrial complex. As noted earlier (in the discussions of *Space Apprentice* and *Hard To Be a God*), gangsterism is closely tied to capitalism in Marxist thought; since both are geared to the accumulation of material wealth to the exclusion of other values, one is considered merely a form of the other. This connection is evident in the behavior of Red and his colleagues and contacts. As stalkers, Red and others fulfill an entrepreneurial function by stealing and making available alien artifacts, a classic case of supply and demand. There is little glory in this grimy, dangerous business; the sole real reward is cash. For this, Red risks death or mutilation, his freedom, and his posterity. By the book's last chapter, virtually all his fellow stalkers in Harmont have met gruesome

ends; the head stalker, a ruthless survivor aptly named Buzzard Bur-
bridge, has lost his legs to witches' jelly, and an associate of Buzzard's,
a once handsome young man, has been reduced to a twisted lump by a
phenomenon of the Zone known as "the meatgrinder." The personal
price Red is paying is summed up in the closing scene of the third
chapter, when the entrepreneur Noonan visits Red's morose family and,
amid forced gaiety, finds himself sharing a table with Red and the
"moulage" of his father.

> Noonan started in on institute business, and while he
> was talking, Monkey appeared noiselessly at the table
> by the old man. She stood there with her hairy paws
> on the table and then in a perfectly childlike way, she
> leaned against the moulage and put her head on his
> shoulder. Noonan went on chatting but thought, as he
> looked at these two horrors born of the Zone: My
> God, what else? What else has to be done to us be-
> fore we understand? Isn't this enough? [Pocket,
> 1977; p. 124].

Nothing stops the greed, however, and in the fourth and closing chapter we watch a hard-bitten Red Schuhart foray into the Zone
with Buzzard's attractive son Arthur (whose birth must have pre-dated
the Visitation) in pursuit of the ultimate prize—a semi-legendary artifact known to the local stalkers as "The Golden Ball." The common
belief is that this globe, which apparently only Buzzard has actually
seen, can grant all the wishes of its possessor. It is thus the consummate symbol of human cupidity. To reach it, Red and Arthur go
through hell, dodging all the familiar dangers only to barely miss being
burned alive by a wandering heat mass, to swim through a body of
stinking green sludge beneath a volley of violet lightning, and finally to
face the old quarry where the Golden Ball lies, with the invisible meatgrinder somewhere in the vicinity. Here is where Red demonstrates
how well he has learned the lessons of his world; using a trick of Buzzard's, he lets the unsuspecting Arthur run right into the violent grasp
of the meatgrinder.

> And the boy kept walking down, dancing a jig,
> shuffling to his own beat, and the white dust rose

from his heels, and he was shouting at the top of his lungs, clearly, joyously, and festively....

And then he was suddenly silent, as though a huge fist had punched him in the mouth. And Redrick saw the transparent emptiness that was lurking in the shadow of the excavator's bucket grab him, throw him up in the air, and slowly slowly twist him, like a housewife wringing her wash. Redrick had time to see one of his dusty shoes fall off his jerking leg and fly high above the quarry. Then he turned away and sat down [p. 151].

With the prospect clear, Red approaches the Golden Ball alone. In trying to formulate his wish, he is torn between his own desires and his angry awareness of the suffering everyone goes through for survival and independence. He is disgusted by the law of the jungle that has turned him into an animal and threatened to turn him into a slave. "God, it's just one long brawl!" he tells himself. In the end, unable to think of anything else, he can only repeat the last words Arthur screamed out before the meatgrinder caught him: "HAPPINESS FOR EVERYBODY, FREE, AND NO ONE WILL GO AWAY UNSATIS-FIED!" These are the last words of the novel.

We never learn whether or not the Golden Ball is capable of granting such a wish. The wish itself, on close examination, proves ambiguous in its import. Though it appears to manifest a degree of altruism unseen elsewhere in the novel, it falls short of the lofty hopes expressed for humanity in other works. Happiness alone is not enough; the electronically drugged hedonists of *The Final Circle of Paradise* had that. Elsewhere in the Strugatsky canon, mankind needs useful work, wisdom, good institutions, and social and scientific progress. On one level, Red's last wish is the desperate cry of a basically good human being who has been ruined by the destructive and dehumanizing values of his society.

Of all the works of the Strugatsky brothers, *Roadside Picnic* provides the strongest criticism of the capitalist ethic. Furthermore, it does so without resorting to the polemicism of earlier works; it proves its point by *showing* rather than *telling*. Structured as a tale of adventure and suspense, it nevertheless functions as a moral tale as well, conveying a familiar message with some disturbing and open-ended touches. For one thing, the story utterly lacks the utopian dreams of other works; even Red's last wish does not offer much of a program for the future. In addition, there is no resolution of man's inept and selfish handling of alien contact; indeed, one could argue—as at least one character does in the novel—that the aliens themselves were inept and selfish in dumping their dangerous garbage on Earth.

In his article on the fairy tale paradigms in the work of the Strugatskys, Csicery-Ronay devotes considerable attention to this short novel. He offers the suggestion, earlier expressed by Stanislaw Lem, that it is a sort of anti-fairy tale, appropriately reflecting the Strugatsky brothers' loss of faith in the utopian hopes that made the fairy tale a suitable model for Soviet fiction. On the other hand, according to this critic, Red's desperate wish for universal happiness indicates that the utopian urge remains; that the Strugatskys do not show the outcome of Red's wish suggests to him—and almost alone to him among the story's analysts—that it could, in fairy tale fashion, come true.

Lem, in his article on *Roadside Picnic* published eventually in *Microworlds*, sees this intersection with the fairy tale as unintentional and a flaw in a work of science fiction. Much of his discussion is given over to some nit-picking on the scientific details of the Visitation, during which he challenges the impression left by the novel that the aliens simply and unthinkingly left their dangerous garbage behind, to be stumbled upon and misused by a non-comprehending humanity. He concludes disapprovingly that "both sides were *meant* to be discredited. Men agree on using the gift only in base and self-destructive ways because that is human nature; and the Senders prove their murderous indifference to humanity because beings of high intelligence do not give a damn about their intellectual inferiors" [Harcourt Brace Jovanovich, 1984; p. 273-274]. This criticism strikes one as odd coming from an author who, in his own "Eighth Voyage" of Ijon Tichy (in *The Star Diaries*) has humanity refused admission to a galactic confederation because its evolution began with the spoiled contents of an alien refrigerator, ejected onto Earth. Perhaps Lem allows such points to be made in satire, but not in a serious work like *Roadside Picnic*.

While Lem does, in general, find the work of the Strugatsky brothers superior to most science fiction, he also generally disapproves of their penchant for social and political discussions. In his own fiction, Lem himself deals almost wholly with scientific and metaphysical questions, many rooted in the difficulty of understanding the cosmos through empirical means. In *Solaris*, for instance, terrestrial scientists spend the better part of a century struggling to comprehend an alien life-form consisting of a neutrino ocean wrapped about a distant planet. In the end, all their theories reflect an automatic and unyielding anthropocentrism. As one cynical and disillusioned Solarist phrases it, "We are only seeking Man. We have no need of other worlds. We need mirrors" [Berkley, 1971; p. 81].

The innate human inability to understand the alien is a major theme—perhaps *the* major theme—of Lem's work of the sixties and seventies, a period during which Lem was among the best-selling and most read authors in the Soviet Union, and a clear influence on the Strugatskys. Indeed, the resurrected corpses of *Picnic* may owe something to Lem's *The Investigation*, which concerns a fruitless endeavor by detectives and scientists to get to the bottom of an inexplicable plague of reanimated corpses.

It is clear in *Roadside Picnic* that humankind is wholly unable to comprehend the alien, and attempts to do so are cut short by human weakness and anthropomorphism—the tendency to see the human face reflected throughout the cosmos. Csicery-Ronay goes so far as to suggest that the aliens show us a humankind of the future, a negative alternative to the positive prognostication offered in the earlier "What You Will Be Like." Lem's influence is, if anything, more evident in the 1976 novel *Za milliard let do kontsa sveta*, literally translated as *A Billion Years Before the End of the World* but published in English as *Definitely Maybe*.

Once again the plot's prime mover is humanity's confrontation with the unknown. As in *Picnic*, the setting is specified, a rare practice in Strugatsky stories with terrestrial locations. This time it is Leningrad in the near future, during an unusually hot summer. The focal character is one Malianov, like Boris Strugatsky an astrophysicist. The novel consists of twelve chapters, put together from twenty-one "excerpts" that begin and end *in medias res*, giving the narrative the hurried, unsettled air of a fever dream.

Early in the story we see Malianov on the verge of a scientific breakthrough regarding curved space. His thoughts and calculations, however, are frequently interrupted by a series of annoying phone calls, wrong numbers all, then by the delivery of an expensive package of liquor and gourmet foods paid for anonymously. At the end of the first chapter, he receives an overnight visit from a beautiful young woman who claims to be an old friend of his vacationing wife; though he keeps the socializing proper, it is a distraction nonetheless. Other interruptions fall rapidly on the heels of this one: a nighttime visit from a mysterious neighbor named Snegovoi, a frightened, ambiguous phone call from Malianov's friend Weingarten, a Kafkaesque early morning invasion by three police officials who accuse Malianov of Snegovoi's murder.

The pieces of the puzzle begin to fall together when Weingarten drops by with a stranger, one Zakhar Gubar, and the latter's ill-behaved boy. It seems that Weingarten, himself a biochemist bent on the Nobel Prize, has recently received a visitation from a little man claiming to be an alien who warned him away from his line of research. Gubar, an inventor, has had his work effectively halted by a sudden onslaught of all the women he has ever known in his life, including one who left behind the boy, supposedly his illegitimate child, along with a warning similar to Weingarten's. The conclusion seems inescapable: someone or something is trying to end their various explorations at the frontiers of knowledge by manipulating their personal lives.

Into this circle Weingarten also drags one Glukhov, an orientalist (like Arkady Strugatsky) who has been prevented from working by debilitating headaches, and Vecherovsky, an acquaintance of all and a superb mathematician. The latter dispassionately and logically attempts to resolve the problem and ends up proving that there *is* no solution as long as they adhere to the belief that an alien conspiracy is holding them at bay. Glukhov proposes that they all abandon their studies, as he has, and enjoy life, whether that means wine, nature, or television.

Up to this point Malianov has been skeptical, unwilling to believe that he and the others have actually been singled out for persecution. He considers his skepticism justified by Vecherovsky's pragmatic reaction until he realizes that Vecherovsky is not so much concerned with the premise—Who is putting on the pressure?—as with the result—How does one choose to behave under it? Glukhov has in fact given up; he is only the squashed, crippled remnant of the man he once was. Rocketry specialist Snegovoi, shot by his own hand, apparently also broke under such pressure. In place of Weingarten's hypothesis of a supercivilization intruding in their work, Vecherovsky proposes a less anthropocentric interpretation of the events: a natural law of "homeostasis" operating in the universe that actually prevents civilizations from becoming supercivilizations and threatening the universe's existence.

When Vecherovsky criticizes Weingarten's theory, he does so in terms reminiscent of Lem. Not only is the idea of a supercivilization too human, it is also typically anthropocentric to think that any super-intelligence worthy of the name could be threatened by mankind at its present stage. To so readily find an anthropomorphic answer to their problem is to fall into the old trap:

> We've rejected God, but we still can't stand on our own two feet without a myth-crutch to hold us up. But we'll have to. We'll have to learn. Because in your situation, not only do you not have any friends, you are so alone that you don't have any enemies, either! [Macmillan, 1978; p. 100-101].

Whatever force is at work, the question is—as Vecherovsky notes—moot. When Malianov tries to fight back by returning to his calculations, events avalanche: his wife comes home in response to an alarming telegram, a full-grown tree suddenly appears the next morning in the courtyard, and Malianov receives a telegram himself reminding him that his son is returning home by plane the next day. Its last two lines are ominous: "BOBCHIK IS SILENT. VIOLATING THE HOMEOSTATIC UNIVERSE" [p. 131]. With that, Malianov collects his notes, puts them in an envelope, and carries them upstairs to Vecherovsky for safe-keeping alongside the work of Weingarten, Gubar, and Glukhov. Vecherovsky's apartment looks as if a bomb had gone off in it, and for the first time Malianov realizes that he has been "under pressure" too. The mathematician has chosen to continue the struggle and to seek others who are similarly minded. He does not expect to defeat the Homeostatic Universe in his lifetime, but, he observes, "There's still a billion years to the end of the world....There's a lot, an awful lot, that can be done in a billion years if we don't give up and we understand, understand and don't give up" [p. 142]. After the ambiguous endings of the last few works, this element of hope amid desperation reminds one of the earlier fiction, such as *Far Rainbow*.

Though in and of itself the concept of a homeostatic universe is intriguing and entertaining, the Western reader cannot avoid reading another level of significance into the novel. The events and much of the rhetoric suggests parallels to intellectual life in a police state. Vecherovsky himself expresses this possibility when he proposes, in jest, that the victimization of his colleagues could be due to "policemen with aberrant behavior patterns" [p. 95]. More direct is the incessant harassment suffered by the characters, harassment that not only stops them from working but leads to spiritual and physical destruction as well. Particularly poignant, in this regard, is what Malianov tells himself after his capitulation.

> The fear, loathing, despair, and feeling of impotence came back, and I realized with unbearable clarity, that from that moment a line of fire and brimstone that could never be crossed was drawn between Vecherovsky and me....And I would never see Weingarten and Zakhar either. We'll have nothing to say to each other; we'll be too embarrassed to meet, nauseated by the sight of each other, and we'll have to buy vodka or port wine to forget the embarrassment and nausea....Bobchik would be alive and well, but he would never grow up to be the man I had wanted him to be. Because I would no longer have the right to want him to be that way. Because he would never be able to be proud of me [p. 138].

Such would indeed be the isolation of the intellectual in a rigidly controlled society. To regard this work solely as a clever and surreptitious attack on the Soviet system, however, would be an act of reductionism. The novel yields its full richness only if placed within the continuum of the Strugatsky's development. *Definitely Maybe* takes the innate conservatism of human institutions, Soviet institutions included, and projects it upon the cosmos. Whereas in earlier works—almost everything from *Hard To Be a God* to *The Ugly Swans*—the committed individual stands alone and at odds with his society, here he finds himself ranged against the entire universe, a universe devoted like the bureaucracies analyzed elsewhere to self-preservation at the expense of progress. If the cosmos itself imitates the inflexibility of governments, perhaps the utopian may be forgiven ineffectiveness and even apostasy. He is hopelessly outnumbered.

At bottom, all the explanations offered by the characters for the occurrences of the novel are constructs of human reason and therefore, by Lem's paradigm, inherently prone to error. A similar theme underlies the remaining stories of the seventies, though in these it is stripped of all political and ideological implications. What is left is a handful of cosmic mystery tales in the Lem vein that lack the depth and resonance of *The Ugly Swans*, *Roadside Picnic*, and the somewhat more whimsical *Definitely Maybe*.　Two of these predate the last-named novel—*Otel' "U pogibshego al'pinista"* (*Hotel "To the Lost Mountaineer"*, 1970) and *Malysh* (*The Kid*, 1973).　Both are novellas, the first dealing with a set of mysterious events finally and somewhat hurriedly explained as the work of robots; it contains minor appearances by Leonid Gorbovsky and other early characters.　The second, published in English as *Space Mowgli*, features a young man raised, like Heinlein's Valentine Michael Smith, by aliens; the mysteries surrounding "the kid" are unconvincingly tied together by the Wanderers, the ancient space race alluded to often in the Strugatskys' early fiction.

　　　The most recent novel of these authors (as of this writing) is also in this cosmic mystery genre, though it is longer and less trivial than those last named.　This is *Zhuk v muraveinike*, published in English as *Beetle in An Anthill*.　Like the other late fiction discussed in this chapter, it touches on the problem of man's tragic misapprehension of the unknown.

　　　One of the real surprises of the novel is its placement in the fictive realm of several earlier works; it brings together the main characters of the 1971 *Prisoners of Power* in the universe of Gorbovsky and Komov.　This blending of worlds works only if one ignores the implications of the earliest fiction, especially the fact that Maxim Kammerer, hero and narrator of *Beetle*, was a superman in *Prisoners*, representative of a stage of humanity only *predicted*, not present, in *Noon*.　There is nothing in *Beetle* of the Maxim who could perceive radiation and survive mortal wounds.　And the Earth of intrigue and suspicion he inhabits is hardly the utopia implied in the earlier fictions.

　　　Perhaps this artistic misjudgment was an attempt on the part of the brothers to appeal to their original fictive universe, as they also did in *Hotel* and *The Kid*, where the moral and political certainties were clearer than in their more mature fiction.　On the other hand, *Beetle* in no way confirms the earlier optimism—quite the contrary.　While primarily a suspense story lacking the literary subtlety of, say, *The Ugly Swans*, it promulgates the darker view of humanity found there.　Indeed, it lacks even the faint spark of hope found in so despairing a work as *Definitely Maybe*.

　　　The book is comprised primarily of a first-person account by Maxim Kammerer, no longer the idealistic naif of *Prisoners* but an agent attached to the bureau that oversees "Progressors," the terrestrial operatives whose job it is to advance historical progress on other planets.　Strannik, the high-ranking Progressor Maxim met on the planet of

Prisoners, is here Maxim's superior, called by the strikingly un-Marxist title "Excellency." He sends Max on an assignment so secret that Max himself does not know its real objective; he only knows he is supposed to locate a Progressor named Lev Abalkin. The details of Max's manhunt alternate, at three points in the narrative, with chapter-length excerpts from Abalkin's report on the investigation of a planet whose native human population has been decimated by non-human aliens. The Wanderers, again, apparently intervened to save the humans from persecution by another race and did so by transporting them to another dimension.

The Wanderers prove to be central in the mystery that surrounds Lev Abalkin. When a world-wide pursuit of the man yields little for Maxim other than that Abalkin has in fact returned to Earth and that the anti-social tendencies of his youth have become more pronounced, Max insists that Excellency inform him of the nature of his quest. It turns out that Abalkin is one of several individuals who grew from a set of human embryos left behind by the Wanderers on a planet that had never known human life. Abalkin, with the products of the other embryos, has remained unaware of his origins until recently and has returned to the Earth for some answers. Excellency, among others, fears the intent of the Wanderers in seeding the Earth's population with these artificial human beings. On the other hand, it is suggested that they may be analogous to the schoolboy experiment of placing a beetle in an anthill just to see what happens. This theory is given support not only by the book's title but by the mark that appeared on Abalkin's arm at puberty, a mark resembling the six-legged Cyrillic letter for *zh*. *Zh* is the first letter of "zhuk," the Russian word for "beetle." Ultimately, no one *can* know for sure what lies behind the action of the aliens. As one character expresses the problem in terms again reminiscent of Lem, "We never will [come up with anything], because the wisest and most experienced of us are still only human" [Macmillan 1980, p. 205].

The indelible mark on Abalkin's arm, like other marks on the arms of the other artifical humans, has a counterpart on one of several coin-shaped artifacts of unknown purpose that were found with the embryos. These objects, known as "detonators" to insiders like Excellency, are hidden in a storeroom in the Museum of Nonterrestrial Civilizations. It is here that all the primary characters come together—Max, Abalkin, Abalkin's former girlfriend, and Excellency, now identified as a one-time scientist named Sikorski—in the climactic final scene. All, including Abalkin, are still ignorant of the alien reason behind the creation of the embryos. As Abalkin searches in bewildered desperation for the detonators in hopes of finding the answer to his existence, Sikorski races to head him off, frightened of the unpredictable consequences. Max catches up to them just as Sikorski shoots Abalkin. The book closes with Abalkin bleeding to death on the floor, the meaning of his life still a mystery—another victim of man's fear of the unknown.

This ending offers no consolations, no promises for the future. Considering the story takes place in the universe of *Noon*, it revokes all the earlier affirmations regarding humankind's moral and intellectual development. Though esthetically less innovative than their best work of the late sixties and seventies, it is at least as radical in its rejection of a single positivistic approach to human nature and human systems. With *Beetle in An Anthill*, the Strugatskys have come full circle to the cosmos of their earliest fiction, but in the meantime they have run the gamut philosophically from a fairly conventional Marxist utopianism, through a doubt-riddled humanism, to a pessimism darkly tinged with disgust.

Patrick McGuire, in his essay on the Strugatskys in *Critical Encounters II*, views this work as expressive of the general Soviet disillusionment, in the time of Brezhnev, with the Marxist expectations of the Khrushchev era. If so, it represents a concomitant disillusionment on the part of the Strugatskys with the potentialities of humankind.

Curiously, the reaction of Soviet readers and critics to the darker world of this novel and its too human characters was not so pessimistic. Vladimir Gakov, in his 1982 panegyric on the Strugatskys, saw Sikorski as a "good man," forced to act against his conscience to avoid a possible risk to all humanity. And in his 1986 interview with Fyodorov, Arkady noted that the members of the Vladivostok Science Fiction Club staged a trial of Sikorski and narrowly acquitted him. If nothing else, such different responses prove that, even in their less ambitious work, the Strugatsky brothers can still stimulate modest controversy.

Humanity's inability to come to terms with the alien in the works of the Strugatskys represents more than the anthropocentric limitation of understanding one finds in Lem. As more political writers, the Strugatskys see in the misapprehension of the unknown an unwillingness in the human mind and spirit to open itself up to new experience, to challenge, and to change. One can look back from *Beetle in An Anthill* to the crass exploitation of the alien in *Picnic*, the mass violence directed against it in *Swans*, and the bureaucratic misuse of it in *Snail* and *Troika* to see how much this failure of understanding and will is connected to the weakness of the individual and the inflexibility of institutions, and to a lack of vision that locks the worst human tendencies into the system, be it Western capitalism or Eastern communism, and locks out the best—the imaginative, the humanist, the progressive. Of course, the alien itself seems at least partly at fault, in being unfeeling, elusive, and intentionally incomprehensible.

As beguiling as is the bright optimism of the earliest work, the late fiction seems wiser and more honest, not to mention more interesting thematically and esthetically. *The Ugly Swans*, *Roadside Picnic*, and, to a lesser extent, *Definitely Maybe* must be considered the climactic works of the career of the brothers Strugatsky.

VI.

CONCLUSION

It should be apparent that a clear set of themes unifies the work of Arkady and Boris Strugatsky. A dominant theme—perhaps *the* dominant one—is the gross disparity between the idealistic hopes for humankind's future, portrayed most vividly in their first phase, and the deep-seated doubts growing out of the empirical observation of human nature. The increasing sorrow, frustration, and anger that infuses the work spanning the decade from the mid-sixties to the mid-seventies reveals the wish to continue to believe in man's potential, but darkened by the fear that the future may turn out to be too much like the present. Along with their heroes like Victor Banev, the Strugatskys lament the individual weakness and institutional inertia that keep the human species from reaching utopia and the stars.

In particular, as science fiction writers they criticize the abuse of science, specifically the misapplication of technology and the search for knowledge, the faulty approach to the unknown, and the waste of human lives and minds. Their fiction is full of scientists ruined by becoming bureaucrats, from the mild case of Yurkovsky in *Space Apprentice* to the Strannik/Excellency/Sikorski figure of *Prisoners* and *Beetle*. The scientist is ideally the archetypal progressive, using imagination, vision, and expertise to expand and improve humanity's cosmos: the bureaucrat, on the other hand, lives to limit, to narrow, and to preserve the status quo. Few reversals could be more tragic than the final act of the former scientist Sikorski, murdering Abalkin out of fear of the unknown.

Of paramount importance to the brothers Strugatsky is the linking of science and morality: the pursuit of knowledge must serve the best interests of mankind. This attitude is summed up in what Darko Suvin has called their "credo":

[Science fiction is] the literature dealing with the
ethics and responsibilities of the scientist [...] with
what those, in whose hands lies the realization of the
highest achievements of human knowledge, feel and
how they relate to their work [...]. Each scientist has
to be a revolutionary humanist, otherwise the inertia
of history will shunt him into the ranks of irresponsi-
ble scoundrels leading the world to its destruction.
[Quoted by Suvin in his Introduction to *The Snail on
the Slope*, p. 19].

The term "revolutionary humanist" is significant. If the Strugatskys are frequently critical of aspects of Soviet society—bureaucratic
rigidity and inefficiency, militarism, and police harassment
(characteristics certainly not unique to the Soviet system)—they are still
decidedly Marxist in their idealism. They continue to hope for a so-
cialist-style world state united in peace, prosperity, and social
progress—classless, egalitarian, and non-competitive. Arkady Strugatsky once stated in an interview in *People's World*: "I never doubted
the correctness of communist ideas although I am not a party member....I acquainted myself with other philosophies[, b]ut none of them
satisfies me as much as communism does."

Even if this statement was made either diplomatically or ironically, it does not refute the essential adherence of the brothers' fiction
to the best hopes of Marxism. Despite their increasing doubts about
human potential and the liberal humanism at the center of their philoso-
phy, it is difficult to see how they could be branded as dissidents by
anyone on either side of the ideological fence.

If they could be guilty of any sin in the eyes of Soviet authority, it would be the unorthodoxy with which they propound these values, together with a reluctant but increasing skepticism directed alike at
institutions, for their innate conservatism, and at the masses, for their
fallibility. As already noted, the Strugatskys' most overt criticisms
came in their satirical fantasies of the late sixties, wherein they came
closest in style to the officially sanctioned satire of *Krokodil*. This was
also the period, between *The Final Circle of Paradise* and *Prisoners of
Power*, when the controversy over the brothers' work loomed largest in
the Soviet press and when they had the most trouble publishing their
work in book form; neither *The Snail on the Slope* nor *The Ugly Swans*
appeared as such in their own country. By no means, however, are

these their most politically controversial works. *Tale of the Troika* savages bureaucracy as least as much as *Snail*, and *The Ugly Swans* stands out more for its harsh realism than any implied political critique of the Soviet system, which is easier to find in the later *Prisoners* and *Definitely Maybe*.

If these two "censored" works—*Snail* and *Swans*—have anything in common, besides the suggestion that revolutionary change may only be accomplished by abandoning our humanity, it is the dark complexity of their vision. In fact, a number of the Strugatskys' strongest critics, among those cited by Suvin in his bibliography, specifically mention the—in their opinion—ambiguous or pessimistic message of these works. In fact, it is striking how similar their complaints are to those being made at the same time by American conservatives about our own unorthodox literature of the sixties, or—more to the point—by the American SF "Old Guard" about the "New Wave" of the decade.

Other evidence suggests that, circa 1969, there was a sharp, widespread cutback in the publishing of Soviet science fiction, even among authors with no history of dealing with political themes. Perhaps the very unconventionality of *Snail* and *Swans qua* science fiction made them easy targets for cancellation; in the USSR, then even more than now, virtually all science fiction was published by presses devoted either to science education or young people. It is difficult, if not impossible, for a Western critic to read the mind of any publisher, let alone a Soviet one, but the history of the Brezhnev regime suggests that decision-making under it was characterized by inefficiency as much as ideological consistency. Arkady Strugatsky himself would be in a good position to know, having been an editor at one of the central SF publishing houses during the period.

The more evidence one takes into account, the harder it is to make the case that the Soviet government has followed a clear-cut policy of suppressing the Strugatskys. The brothers themselves have certainly denied as much, and the fact of their persistent prominence in Soviet publications tends to corroborate them. On the other hand, their literary colleague, critic Yuli Kagarlitsky, has observed that the controversies over their work have left them exhausted and dispirited. He also notes that, in the age of *glasnost* and *perestroika*, there is not enough book-quality paper in the Soviet Union to keep up with the demand for their fiction.

Unfortunately, the Strugatskys' work of the eighties pales before their fiction of the sixties and seventies. Though they contributed to *The Stalker*, the Soviet movie version of *Roadside Picnic*, the film lacks the sense of the alien and the implied critique of human greed that makes the novella so interesting. Another film, *Magicians*, and some shorter works published recently in Soviet periodicals return to some of their oldest and least controversial themes. "Five Spoonfuls of Elixir," for instance, a short screenplay featured in the 1986 number of *Soviet Literature* that also contains Arkady's interview with Gyodorov, concerns a writer who is offered immortality provided he commits homocide; as a good Strugatsky hero, he of course values human life over everything and turns the offer down.

The esthetic malaise in their latest work reflects a broader trend in Soviet science fiction, which since the sixties has veered increasingly away from experimental forms and themes. Again, some have charged official suppression of the genre, reminiscent of but not as rigorous as the purges of the Stalin era. But others have pointed to the more universal tendency toward creative cycles in SF. After all, American science fiction has itself settled down considerably since the radical experimentation of the New Wave sixties. If we do not have the specter of a totalitarian state authority choosing which books see print and which do not, the democratic forces of popular taste and marketplace values have imposed their own conservative restraints on the SF imagination.

Indeed, circa 1980 a concerted economic and esthetic retrenchment in SF publishing drove the last, most visible remnants of the New Wave out of the American marketplace: in one blow the two most distinguished New Wave anthologies, Damon Knight's *Orbit* and Robert Silverberg's *New Dimensions*, disappeared, and prominent New Wave figures like J. G. Ballard found themselves unable to publish in the United States; he would not reappear on bookstore shelves on this side of the Atlantic until his realistic novel *Empire of the Sun*, backed by Spielberg's movie version, granted him international status. Other similarly daring writers who rose to prominence in the sixties—Samuel Delany, Thomas Disch, Norman Spinrad, Barry Malzberg—can barely remain in print today.

In fact, if Soviet publishing has not always done justice to the work of the Strugatskys, the American marketplace has certainly failed to give them the audience they deserve. Patrick McGuire laments, justly, that their work regularly reached English readers a decade after its original appearance. In the world of science fiction, a decade significantly dates a work; what was innovative in 1960 was not in 1970.

While much of the delay can be ascribed to the sluggishness of Soviet-American publishing negotiations, the sad fact is that the average American science fiction fan, and the average publisher who services him, shows little interest in SF outside the Anglo-American tradition. Macmillan/Collier merits considerable praise for their active program of the late seventies and early eighties in publishing the works of the Strugatskys and other Soviet SF authors, but in the end the marketplace could not justify it; for the most part, the fiction in question quickly went out of print, a victim of mediocre sales.

Now, at the beginning of the nineties, one must search hard through used book stores and libraries to find the works of the Strugatsky brothers. For serious SF fan and serious SF scholar alike, however, the search is well worth the trouble. The Strugatsky canon is an impressive one—rich, varied, and intelligent, if occasionally uneven. If one wished to limit one's reading to the best or most representative of their work, I would recommend the following:

1. From the earliest phase, *Noon: 22nd Century*, for its bright, humane depiction of the future; and *Far Rainbow*, for its attractively packaged warning about the consequences of unrestrained scientific research and its portrayal of simple heroism in the face of tragedy;

2. From the Brothers' second period, *Hard To Be a God*, for its fast-moving plot and vivid characters; and *Prisoners of Power*, for its artfully depressing commentary on our times;

3. Of the fantasies, *The Second Invasion from Mars*, for its wit and economy; and *The Snail on the Slope*, for its remarkable imagery and complexity;

4. Finally, *The Ugly Swans*, *Roadside Picnic*, and *Definitely Maybe*, representing the esthetic and thematic high points of the latter half of their career.

It is hard to imagine where the Strugatskys can go from here, especially considering the marks of creative exhaustion in their latest fiction. But even if they never again approach the level of their best work, enough exists already to keep the critical reader busy for some time.

BIBLIOGRAPHICAL NOTES

I. Works by the Strugatskys in English

Beetle in an Anthill. New York: Macmillan, 1980.

Definitely Maybe. New York: Macmillan, 1978 (Collier, 1978).

"Destination: Amaltheia," in *Destination: Amaltheia* (an anthology). Moscow: Foreign Languages Publishing House, 1962.

"An Emergency Case," in *Path Into the Unknown*, ed. by Judith Merril. New York: Delacorte, 1968. London: McGibbon & Kee, 1968.

Escape Attempt. New York: Macmillan, 1982.

Far Rainbow. Moscow: Mir, 1967. New York: Macmillan, 1979 (Collier, 1980); in one volume with *The Second Invasion from Mars*.

The Final Circle of Paradise. New York: DAW, 1976. London: Dobson, 1976.

["Irene"] "From Beyond," in *Soviet Literature* (no. 1, 1982): 8-36.

"The Gigantic Fluctuation," in *Journey Across Three Worlds*. Moscow: Mir, 1973. Incorporated into Chapter 10 of *Space Apprentice*.

Hard To Be a God. New York: Seabury, 1973; DAW, 1974. London: Eyre Methuen, 1975.

Monday Begins on Saturday. New York: DAW, 1977.

Noon: 22nd Century. New York: Macmillan, 1977 (Collier, 1979).

Prisoners of Power. New York: Macmillan, 1977 (Collier, 1978).

Roadside Picnic. New York: Macmillan, 1977; Pocket Books, 1978 (with *Tale of the Troika*). London: Gollancz, 1978; Penguin, 1982. New York: Pocket Books (Timescape), 1982.

The Second Martian Invasion. In *Vortex*, ed. by C. G. Bearne. London: MacGibbon & Kee, 1970; Pan, 1971. As *The Second War of the Worlds*: New York: Macmillan, 1973. As *The Second Invasion from Mars*, in one volume with *Far Rainbow*: New York: Macmillan, 1979 (Collier, 1980).

"Six Matches," in *The Heart of the Serpent* (an anthology). Moscow: Foreign Languages Publishing House, 1962. *More Soviet Science Fiction*. New York: Collier, 1962. *Soviet Literature* (no. 5, 1968).

The Snail on the Slope. New York: Bantam, 1980 (but withdrawn almost immediately from publication). London: Gollancz, 1980.

Space Apprentice. New York: Macmillan, 1981.

"Spontaneous Reflex," in *A Visitor from Outer Space* (an anthology). Moscow: Foreign Languages Publishing House, 1962. *Soviet Science Fiction*. New York: Collier, 1962.

Tale of the Troika. New York: Macmillan, 1977; Pocket Books, 1978 (in one volume with *Roadside Picnic*).

The Time Wanderers. London: Richardson & Steirman, 1987. New York: St. Martin's Press, 1988.

The Ugly Swans. New York: Macmillan, 1979 (Collier, 1980).

"Wanderers and Travelers," in *Path Into the Unknown*, cited above. A different translation of "Pilgrims and Wanderers," published in *Noon*.

"The White Cone of Alaid," in *Last Door to Aiya*, ed. by Mirra Ginsburg. New York: S. G. Phillips, 1968.

II. Background and Selected Criticism

Brandis, E. and V. Dmitrevsky. "In the Land of Science Fiction." *Soviet Literature* 5 (1968). Reprinted in *Soviet Science Fiction*, cited above.

Csicery-Ronay, István, Jr. "Towards the Last Fairy Tale: On the Fairy-Tale Paradigm in the Strugatskys' Science Fiction, 1963-1972." *Science-Fiction Studies* 13 (March 1986): 1-41.

Fyodorov, Alexander. "Arkadi Strugatsky: 'Man Must Always Be Man.'" *Soviet Literature* 9 (1983): 113-123.

Gakov, Vladimir. "A Test of Humanity: About the Work of the Strugatsky Brothers." *Soviet Literature* 1 (1982): 154-161.

Greene, Diana. "Male and Female in *The Snail on the Slope* by the Strugatsky Brothers." *Modern Fiction Studies* 32 (Spring 1986): 97-108).

Griffiths, John. *Three Futures: American, British, and Soviet Science Fiction*. Totowa, NJ: Barnes & Noble, 1980.

Lem, Stanislaw. "About the Strugatskys' Roadside Picnic." *Science-Fiction Studies* 10 (November 1984): 291-303. Reprinted in *Microworlds* (San Diego: Harcourt Brace, 1984; 243-278).

McGuire, Patrick L. "Future History, Soviet Style: The Work of the Strugatsky Brothers," in *Critical Encounters II: Writers and Themes in Science Fiction*, ed. by Tom Staicar. New York: Ungar, 1982, p. 104-124.

_____. "Russian SF," in *Anatomy of Wonder*, 2nd ed., ed. by Neil Barron. New York: Bowker, 1981.

Salvestroni, Silvonetta. "The Ambiguous Miracle in Three Novels by the Strugatsky Brothers." *Science-Fiction Studies* 11 (November 1984): 291-303.

Silin, G. "Why Science Fiction Is Not Free." *Soviet Studies in Literature*, 14 (1978): 48-54.

Suvin, Darko. "Criticism of the Strugatskii Brothers' Work." *Canadian-American Slavic Studies* 6 (Summer 1972): 286-307.

_____. *Russian Science Fiction, 1956-1974: A Bibliography*. Elizabethtown, NY: Dragon Press, 1976.

_____. "Russian SF and Its Utopian Tradition," Chapter 11 of *Metamorphoses of Science Fiction*. New Haven, Yale University Press, 1979.

_____. "The Literary Opus of the Strugatskii Brothers." *Canadian-American Slavic Studies* 8 (Fall 1974): 454-463.

"A Talk with Arkadi Strugatsky." *Soviet Literature* (no. 12, 1986): 36-40.

ABOUT STEPHEN W. POTTS

Stephen W. Potts received his Ph.D. in English from the University of California at Berkeley in 1980, before spending a year as a Fulbright Fellow teaching American literature in Germany. That year also saw the publication of his first scholarly article (on Stanislaw Lem), and his first fiction sale (to Robert Silverberg's SF anthology, *New Dimensions 10*). He has since published two monographs on Joseph Heller—including *From Here to Absurdity: The Moral Battlefields of Joseph Heller*, Volume 36 in The Milford Series—as well as articles on F. Scott Fitzgerald and a number of American, British, and Slavic science fiction authors. He is currently conducting courses in science fiction, popular culture, and creative writing at the University of California at San Diego, while marketing a novel through literary agent Richard Curtis, and completing a critique on the work of F. Scott Fitzgerald for The Borgo Press.

INDEX

www.ingramcontent.com/pod-product-compliance
Lightning Source LLC
LaVergne TN
LVHW091202080426
835509LV00006B/789